SLADE

Stanwyck Park isn't the most exciting of places and Eddie has long since given up hope of anything interesting happening there. But little does he know that on this particular afternoon that's where he will meet a most unusual person. A man appears in a clearing and introduces himself as Slade. He looks just like a sailor – but there's something very odd about him. He doesn't seem to belong in the twentieth century – it's almost as if he's from another planet, although that idea is just too bizarre! But Slade doesn't seem to understand things like tin cans and supermarkets, money and work!

Then even stranger things start to happen – there are foreign voices coming out of his cap, and he can look into the past *and* the future. Eddie begins to wonder where on earth Slade comes from, and the answer which always comes to his mind is . . . nowhere on earth!

This must be the most exciting thing that's ever happened to Eddie – but there are more adventures to come . . .

John Tully left school at fifteen and joined a local newspaper, later becoming a reporter for a national paper. He now writes for children and young people and has dramatized many well-known children's novels for television, as well as writing film scripts and original television plays of his own.

SLADE

John Tully

PUFFIN BOOKS

Puffin Books, Penguin Books Ltd, Harmondsworth, Middlesex, England
Viking Penguin Inc., 40 West 23rd Street, New York, New York 10010, U.S.A.
Penguin Books Australia Ltd, Ringwood, Victoria, Australia
Penguin Books Canada Ltd, 2801 John Street, Markham, Ontario, Canada L3R 1B4
Penguin Books (N.Z.) Ltd, 182–190 Wairau Road, Auckland 10, New Zealand

First published by Methuen Children's Books Ltd 1985
Published in Puffin Books 1987

Printed and bound in Great Britain by
Cox & Wyman Ltd, Reading

For Diana

ONE

Eddie was wandering alone through the wood at the end of Stanwyck Park because he had nothing better to do that afternoon. When he had first explored the wood as a young child he had thought it a mysterious place, but at thirteen he'd given up hope of anything exciting happening there.

Just as he was thinking this, a strange breeze whistled through the trees. It stirred the dry leaves on the path and blew Eddie's hair into his eyes. It was uncannily hot, almost burning his cheeks. Then, just as suddenly, it died down and the air grew cool again.

Eddie moved cautiously in the direction the breeze had come from and stopped on the edge of the clearing in the middle of the wood.

A young man stood on the sunlit turf, tall and strongly built, his features regular, his skin lightly tanned. He looked like a sailor in his white slacks and blue blazer, with a yachting cap on his head, a camera slung over his shoulder and a kit-bag resting on the ground beside him.

He was turning round slowly, examining his

surroundings intently, and his lips moved as if he were talking softly to himself.

Seeing Eddie, he looked startled, then smiled cheerfully. 'Hello?' he said. 'How are you? Nice to meet!' He had a foreign accent that was hard to pin down.

Eddie took a step backwards, having no wish to get involved with a strange foreigner.

'I am Slade,' said the man. 'What is your name?'

Still Eddie didn't answer.

'I am looking for food and sheltering. Where to find you can tell me, please?'

Looking for food and shelter in Stanwyck Park? The man was obviously nuts.

Slade hitched his kit-bag over his shoulder, stepping forward, and Eddie bolted through the trees, back to the safety of the lawns and gravel paths. He hid behind the bowling-pavilion and waited.

A few minutes later Slade came out of the wood, gazing at the people in deck-chairs and the children playing, as if he had never seen such things before. Then he set off down the path towards the main gate and Eddie followed him at a prudent distance.

Slade carried on through the gateway, paused again to stare at everything in sight, and took another step forward, into the roadway. A lorry sounded its horn and he stepped back hastily. After this he set off more cautiously, along the pavement.

When he reached the High Street he stopped again, surveying the shops, the traffic and the bustling crowd. He spotted an empty bus shelter and hurried towards it.

As Eddie watched in astonishment, Slade dumped his kit-bag inside the shelter and moved on down the street, pausing every now and then to look into the shop windows. Not once did he glance back at his kit-bag. Didn't he care about it? Didn't he want it any more?

Eddie slipped into the bus shelter and stared at the bag. What did a mad foreigner carry in his luggage? Not a bomb or he'd be hurrying away, not strolling down the street window-gazing.

The bag was fastened at the top by a cord passed through rings and knotted. Eddie bent down to undo the knot, but it was a lot tighter than he had expected. Better not fiddle with it in the street, he decided. Of course he should hand it to the police. Surely there was no harm in taking it home first, to have a quick look inside ...?

The doorbell of Number 22 Latimer Road chimed, again and again. Janet Salter left the half-peeled potatoes in the sink and went to answer it. Eddie was outside with a pale green kit-bag beside him.

'Left my key in my other jeans,' Eddie explained. He hoisted the bag into the hall and began to drag it up the stairs.

'Where did you get that?' asked Janet suspiciously, planting her hands on her ample hips.

'From a kid I know. Some junk his dad threw out.'

9

Janet frowned. 'We've enough junk in this house already.'

'I'll chuck out anything I don't want.'

'I know you will – all over the floor! I'm sick of clearing up after you. And while I think of it –'

But the door of Eddie's room closed behind him.

He sat on his bed, pulled the bag towards him and tugged at the knot. The loops stayed as firm as welded steel.

He took his penknife from his pocket and sawed at the thin cord. The blade had no effect. Impatiently, he brought the point of the knife down on the side of the canvas bag. There was a sharp 'ping' and the blade snapped in two.

Eddie's fingers tingled from the shock but there was not a dent, not a scratch on the bag. What kind of canvas was this?

Several minutes later he was still staring at it, baffled, when the doorbell chimed again. He went out of his room and peeped down the stairs to see his mother go to the door.

A cheerful voice spoke, 'Hello? How are you? Nice to meet.'

Eddie sucked in his breath in dismay. He had looked back several times on his way home to make sure no one was following him.

'Beg your pardon?' said Janet.

'I am looking, please, for a boy with my bagging.'

'Boy with what?'

'My bagging. It is this high and round like this. I

put it in a sheltering in the street. Then I go to look for foods. When I come back the bagging is gone.'

'Is it ... green?' asked Janet, her voice growing tight.

'Green, yes! When I find it is gone I look backwards to find out what has happened.'

'Look backwards?' asked Janet, puzzled.

'Ten minutes back. I see the boy taking the bag and I follow him here.'

'I don't quite understand,' admitted Janet, 'but I think I've seen your bag. Please come in.'

Slade followed Janet into the front room.

Feeling sick, Eddie fetched the bag from his room. He was heaving it down the stairs when Janet came back to the hall. The look she gave him from weary eyes told him what she thought of him.

He dragged the bag into the front room where Slade was examining the striped wallpaper and the faded furniture. Seeing Eddie he smiled as cheerfully as ever. 'Hello? Nice to meet again.'

'This is my son, Eddie,' said Janet grimly. 'Is this your bag?'

'Yes. That is my bagging – bag.' He turned to Eddie. 'Tell me, please, why did you abscond it?'

'Why did I what?'

'Why did you take it!' said Janet angrily.

'Didn't want to leave it there, did I, in case someone nicked it.' Eddie ducked the swipe which Janet aimed at his head. 'I was going to hand it over to the cops – straight up!'

'I've had trouble with him ever since his dad died,' sighed Janet. 'Eddie was only a nipper then. I've tried psychology. I've tried reasoning. I've tried tanning the hide off him. None of it does any good. You can wallop him yourself if you like.'

'Hang about!' said Eddie, alarmed.

'There, you see? He's more scared of you.'

'Scared of me?' Slade sounded upset. 'Please, I wish to hurt no one.'

'That's all right then,' said Eddie, relieved.

'It's *not* all right!' said Janet angrily. 'Tell him you're very sorry.'

'Sorry,' grunted Eddie.

'Are you going to call the police?' asked Janet anxiously.

'Police? What is police?' asked Slade.

'He doesn't know!' whispered Eddie.

'Perhaps we can make up for it in some way,' suggested Janet with relief. 'Is there anything we can do to help you?'

Slade looked grateful. 'You can tell me, please, where I can find foods?'

'Of course,' said Janet. 'There's a supermarket round the corner. Eddie can show you. He can help you find what you want.'

Janet glanced at Eddie who nodded, glad that his punishment would be no more than a trudge round the supermarket.

'You can leave your bag here if you like,' Janet went on. 'It'll save you lugging it round the shop.'

'Thank you, most kind,' said Slade.

Slade eyed the customers picking goods off the shelves. 'Is most interesting,' he observed. 'People take what is needful to them, like we do.'

Eddie handed him a basket. 'What do you want from here?'

Slade looked about him, unsure. 'If *you* want foods, what do you take?'

'Mum does all the shopping. Have you got anywhere to cook things?'

'Cook? I think not.'

'So you want stuff that's ready to eat. Like this.' Eddie offered him a can of corned beef.

'Is very hard,' said Slade, tapping the can. 'How do you eat it?'

'You have to open it first!'

'Ah! Now I cotton. The foods are inside?'

'Haven't you seen tinned food before?' asked Eddie, incredulous. 'Where do you come from?'

Slade ignored the question. 'Let us make more choosings.'

'D'you like tea or coffee?'

'I don't know.'

Eddie gave up asking questions. He shoved goods into the basket till it was full. 'Is that enough?' he asked.

Slade looked at the basket. 'When it is full, that is my share, yes?'

'What do you mean, share? Have more if

13

you want.'

Slade shook his head. 'Always give more than you take from. That is the say-so of the Great Alph.'

'Great who?'

'No matter,' said Slade quickly. 'Shall we make departure?'

'Sure. Let's go.'

Slade marched swiftly down the aisle, past the girl at the cash desk and out into the street.

'Hey!' called Eddie, running after him.

The girl watched them go, wide-eyed, then called out, 'Mr Ferguson!'

'What's the big idea?' asked Eddie when he caught up with Slade.

'I pardon you?'

'You haven't paid for that!' Seeing Slade's blank look, Eddie added firmly, 'You must know what paying means.'

Slade nodded. 'One pays respect to other persons. One pays the community with service.'

'You're supposed to pay for the food, with money!'

'Money? What is money?'

Eddie glared at him. 'I don't believe it! You're a bigger tealeaf than I am.'

Slade shook his head helplessly. 'There is much in your speaking I do not cotton.'

Eddie looked over his shoulder. The girl had come out of the supermarket with a tight-suited young man at her side. She pointed at Eddie and Slade.

'Run for it!' said Eddie.

'I pardon you?'

'Don't pardon me – run!' He gave Slade a shove to start him moving.

'Stop you two!' yelled Ferguson as he gave chase.

'This way!' said Eddie, turning down a side street.

'Please explain this proceeding,' said Slade. 'I wish to do what is rightful, but why are we running?'

'Because that bloke is trying to catch us.'

Slade looked over his shoulder as Ferguson came round the corner. 'If he wishes to catch us, why do we not stop?'

'You're loco,' said Eddie. 'Plain loco!'

Eddie turned again down a narrow alley and paused at the end of it. 'We'll split up. You go that way. Don't let him catch you or you'll be in trouble.'

Slade trotted off as he was told, clutching the basket of food. Eddie crossed the road heading in the opposite direction. Reaching another corner he stopped to look back.

Slade had disappeared from view. Ferguson reached the end of the alley and spotted Eddie. 'Hi!' he shouted, giving chase again.

Eddie darted round the corner and dodged behind a parked lorry halfway down the street. As Ferguson dashed past, Eddie circled round the lorry and headed back again the way he had come. A moment later he heard Ferguson's footsteps halt ... and start back again after him.

Eddie's legs were weary and he was getting short of breath. Ferguson was catching up with him. He felt a bitter sense of injustice. Why should he be caught when Slade was to blame?

Rounding the corner once more, he saw Slade standing in a doorway on the other side of the street. The basket was at his feet and he was raising his camera to his eye. Crazy nit! What a time to be taking snapshots!

What followed was even more surprising. For a brief moment a purple light, sharp as a laser beam, flashed from the lens of the camera. It shot past Eddie and, almost at once, the sound of Ferguson's footsteps behind him changed from a fast clatter to a slow, measured tread.

Eddie looked over his shoulder. Ferguson was still making the movements of a man running fast, yet he was travelling in long, loping strides, like an athlete seen in slow motion on a TV screen.

Bewildered but thankful, Eddie veered across the road. Slade picked up the basket and they set off together at a brisk trot. Ferguson was left far behind, sailing over the ground like a ship on an ocean swell.

'What's happened to him?' asked Eddie.

'His time-curve is flattened,' said Slade.

'Time-curve?'

'So he will not catch us. All is right now, is it not?'

'All right for us,' agreed Eddie. 'Bit dodgy for him, if he's going to lope around like that for ever.'

Slade shook his head. 'Time-curves are elastic. Soon he will be as normal again.'

Ferguson was out of sight and they slowed down to a walk.

'How did you do it?' asked Eddie, glancing at the camera.

'I cannot talk about it more,' said Slade.

TWO

Janet took the goods out of the wire basket, checking the prices.

'I make it £15.80,' she said. She took the money from her purse and showed it to Slade. 'Ten pounds, five pounds, fifty pence, those are tenpence each. I'll go round to Bateson's and pay for this myself!'

'When you take from the shop you give them pieces of paper and metal? Why?'

'So the shop can pay the people who work there,' said Eddie impatiently.

'Like I get paid for working at the coffee bar,' said Janet. She eyed Slade, deeply puzzled. 'I didn't think there was anywhere on earth where they don't use money nowadays. Where *do* you come from?'

Slade looked uncomfortable. 'Please, I cannot tell you. If I do there will be much fuss and I cannot carry on my mission.'

'What mission?' asked Janet.

'I come to make research.'

'Are you a spy?' asked Janet, dismayed.

'If he was a spy he'd have a proper cover story,' said Eddie, 'and money too.'

'I have caused you much disturbing,' said Slade apologetically. 'I will make departure now.'

'Where will you go?' asked Janet.

'I found sheltering in the street. I will go there.'

'That was a bus shelter!' exclaimed Eddie. 'You can't stay there. You'll have to go to a hotel.'

'How can he, with no money?' Janet glanced at Slade who looked as helpless as a lost dog, and compassion got the better of her. 'You can stay here just for tonight. You can sleep in the front room.'

Eddie spent a restless night thinking about Slade. An idea came into his mind, so bizarre that he thrust it aside and finally he fell asleep, to dream about time-curves.

It was barely light when he woke up. He dressed at once and crept downstairs. He opened the door of the front room and peeped inside.

Slade was asleep on the bed-settee, his clothes neatly folded on a chair beside him. His cap lay on the pillow by his head.

The camera stood on the sideboard. Eddie tiptoed into the room and picked it up, looking at it closely in a slice of light that came through a gap in the curtains. It seemed to be an ordinary model.

'Good daytime, Eddie.'

Eddie jumped. 'Nice camera,' he said guiltily, putting it back on the sideboard. 'Did you sleep well?'

Slade rubbed his eyes. 'Yes, I think I sleep well. Is there something you wish?'

'I came to . . . to ask what you'd like for breakfast.'

'Breakfast?' Slade considered this. 'I have what you have.'

'O.K. D'you know where to wash and all that?'

'Your mother has showed me — how to turn the taps.'

Eddie had the breakfast things laid out on the kitchen table when Slade came in dressed in his yachting gear, complete with cap.

'You shouldn't wear your cap indoors,' said Eddie.

Slade took the cap off reluctantly. 'If I do not wear it they will not see . . .' He stopped. 'No matter. I must do what is right.'

'I'll hang it up for you,' said Eddie. He examined the cap as he took it into the hall. It had an ornate badge on the front and thick lining inside. He hung it on the hall stand and went back to the kitchen.

'Must we call you Slade?' he asked as he poured crispies into two bowls. 'Don't you have a first name?'

Slade thought about this for a moment. 'At home my name is Alph Uro.'

'So we can call you Alf, O.K.?'

'If you wish.'

They had finished their breakfast when Janet came downstairs, surprised to see her son up so early.

'Morning, Mr Slade,' she said.

'He's called Alf,' said Eddie.

Janet poured herself coffee and sat at the table.

Slade pushed his empty bowl aside and put a hand into his jacket. He brought out a large translucent

20

stone set in a pale blue circle and laid it on the table. The stone glinted sharply in the light.

'This is what we call an Eye of Alph,' he said.

Janet's eyes widened. 'It's beautiful! What kind of stone is it?'

'Is carbon crystal,' said Slade. 'We have many such at home.'

'Crystal?' said Janet, uncertain. 'I thought for a moment it was ... Never mind, it's very lovely. I'm sure you could get some money for it.'

'Money?' Slade shook his head. 'I wish to give it to you.'

Janet caught her breath. 'It's very kind of you, but you must have money to live on. Take it to Mr Jameson in York Road. He buys all kinds of jewellery and things. Please do it, for my sake, Mr Slade ... I mean, Alf.'

When Slade had left the house Eddie went up to his room, thoughtful. Something was nagging at the back of his mind. At last he had an idea. He dived under his bed and dragged out the battered hold-all which contained his schoolbooks, stuffed away for the summer holidays. He found a chemistry book and looked up the chapter on 'Carbon'.

Then he bounded down the stairs and dived out of the front door.

The shop was crammed with bric-à-brac piled on shelves and tables. Jameson stood behind the counter examining the Eye of Alph through a jeweller's eyeglass. He was a tubby little man with shiny pink cheeks and small, shrewd eyes.

He glanced sideways at Slade. 'I'll give you twenty-five pounds.' Getting no reaction he added, 'It's not really worth that much.'

'If it is worth not so much you should give me less,' said Slade.

Jameson's eyebrows rose but he quickly recovered. 'Sid Jameson never goes back on his word.' He opened a cash box and handed Slade two ten pound notes and a five pound note.

'I thank you most kindly,' said Slade.

'If you've got any more little knick-knacks be sure to bring them to me.'

The bell over the street door tinkled loudly as Eddie rushed into the shop. 'Alf, hang about –!' He stopped, seeing the notes in Slade's hand. 'Have you sold it already?'

Slade nodded. 'Mr Jameson has give me twenty-five pounds.'

Eddie's face twisted in pain. 'Do you know what carbon crystal is? It's *diamond*!' He pointed a finger at the Eye of Alph. 'A diamond that big must be worth a fortune!'

Jameson swept the jewel from the counter and put it in his pocket. 'You took the money,' he said to Slade. 'The deal is concluded.'

'You've cheated him!' said Eddie.

Jameson's pink cheeks turned bright red and his voice became shrill. 'How dare you accuse me of cheating!' As he spoke his finger slid under the counter, pressing a button.

'Please, what is cheated?' asked Slade.

'Conned, ripped-off, taken to the cleaners!' said Eddie, furious. He turned to Jameson again. 'Is it a diamond or isn't it?'

'It is a diamond,' said Jameson, controlling his voice, 'but it has a crack in it. That's why it's not worth much.'

A curtain covering a doorway at the back of the shop was thrust aside and a grizzly bear appeared.

At second glance Eddie decided it was not a grizzly bear. The bulky man, whose frame filled the doorway, had whiskers over most of his face, and down his massive chest, where his shirt hung open.

'There's a customer complaining, Harry,' said Jameson.

Harry shambled up to the counter glowering at them.

'Hello? How are you? Nice to meet,' said Slade.

Eddie knew when he was beaten. 'Come on, Alf,' he said. 'Let's make departure.'

The doorbell tinkled as they left the shop.

They walked slowly down York Road, both deep in thought.

'Crack there cannot be in the Eye of Alph,' said Slade at last. 'Our people choose most carefully such stones. Mr Jameson has made mistake.'

Eddie stopped abruptly. 'Mistake, my foot! He

was lying!'

'What is lying?'

'Lying is telling you it was worth twenty-five pounds when he knows it's worth a hundred times as much, maybe more.'

Slade shook his head. 'How can a person say something he knows is not true?'

Eddie wanted to cry out in frustration. 'What's the good of arguing about it now?'

But Slade wasn't listening. 'I must go back and tell him he is mistaken, so that he can put right what is wrongful.'

'You're joking! He'll set Harry on you.'

'Set him on? What does that mean?'

'It means lam, bash, wallop, thud,' said Eddie, striking his fist into his palm.

'What strange proceeding,' said Slade. 'I do not wish to lambash this Harry.'

'Lambash *him*? He'll slaughter *you*!'

'When justice has been undone it must be done up again,' said Slade firmly. 'The Great Alph says so.'

'Then let *him* fight Harry,' said Eddie.

But Slade was already marching briskly down the street.

Jameson came from the back of the shop in answer to the bell. Seeing Slade and Eddie, the welcoming smile disappeared.

'What are you doing here?' he asked.

Eddie stayed near the door for a quick getaway but

Slade went up to the counter. 'Please to understand, Mr Jameson, crack there is not in the Eye of Alph.'

'I'm not going to argue about that,' said Jameson stiffly. 'It's my problem now.'

Slade seemed puzzled. 'But I only wish to make correction.' He put the banknotes on the counter. 'Please to return the Eye.'

Jameson raised his voice a fraction, 'Harry!'

The curtain behind him was pushed aside and Harry loomed into view.

'This gent does not know when a deal is a deal. Kindly make it clear to him.'

Harry nodded and shambled forwards.

'Not in here,' added Jameson, glancing round the cluttered shop. 'Outside.'

'Watch it, Alf,' warned Eddie.

'I understand,' said Slade sadly. 'Harry wishes to make lambash.' He took a step backwards, raising the camera to his eye.

Harry was on his way round the end of the counter. Seeing the camera pointed at him he let out a bellow of rage and launched himself across the shop floor with surprising speed for such a heavy man.

Slade pressed the button and the purple flash stabbed from the lens of the camera. For a brief moment Harry was outlined in a faint purple haze. His pace changed in mid-stride. Instead of thundering at Slade like a juggernaut lorry he floated across the floor, more like a drifting balloon.

'Flattened his time-curve!' breathed Eddie in awe.

25

Slade waited till the big man was an arm's length away, then stepped to one side. Harry went past him, carried on at the same majestic pace by his own momentum, till he blundered into a stack of shelves which gave way under the impact. Bowls and vases crashed to the floor.

Jameson gave a cry of horror. 'You clumsy fool! What d'you think you're doing?'

'Please,' said Slade, 'let us now agree what is proper to do.'

But Jameson was concerned only with Harry. 'I told you to get him out of here!'

Harry heaved himself round, a look of bewilderment on his face. His eyes focused on Slade and he hurled himself forward. That is, his legs and arms pumped with effort but he made no more speed than a funeral march.

'Get a move on, can't you?' hissed Jameson.

'Consider what happens when justice is misdone,' said Slade, stepping aside to allow Harry to motor past him. 'The world is made poorer. Hurt and painfulness are spread and –'

He was interrupted by loud clattering as Harry collided with a table and bulldozed it along in front of him amid a trail of china statuettes.

'Great oaf!' shrieked Jameson, putting his hands to his head.

'Please do not be angered with your friend,' said Slade. 'His time-curve is warped. Return my carbon crystal and all will be harmonised.'

26

At last Jameson abandoned faith in Harry and turned to Slade. 'You can't do this to me. Business is business!'

'What is business?' asked Slade.

'Look out,' said Eddie. 'Harry's setting sail again.'

Harry was charging for the third time like an angry elephant with gout. He was trying to say something too, but the sounds, drawn out in a tone as deep as a foghorn, meant nothing to his listeners.

Jameson turned anxiously. 'No, Harry!' he pleaded. 'Not again. Stop, please!' He raised his hands as if to restrain Harry with his own puny strength. Eddie had a vision of a child trying to halt a charging rhinoceros.

Just as Jameson was about to be trampled underfoot Slade reached out and hauled him to safety.

This time Harry tried to turn sideways but the attempt only unbalanced him.

'No!' Jameson put his hands over his eyes.

Harry staggered slowly backwards into the flimsy partition which covered the rear of the shop window. There was a loud noise of splintering wood, followed by a terrible clatter of glass, metal and china as he landed on the window display.

While the others stared at him he sat up slowly. The fury had been knocked out of him and only bafflement remained.

Jameson put a shaking hand in his pocket, took out the Eye of Alph and handed it to Slade. 'Take it! Get out of here. And don't ever come back!'

When Janet returned from the coffee bar, after serving lunches, there was no sign of Eddie or Slade, but the kit-bag was still in the front room. She was half-way up the stairs with the vacuum cleaner when the front door opened and Eddie came in with a dazed look on his face, Slade behind him.

'Eleven thousand, Mum!' Eddie's voice trembled. 'They gave him eleven thousand quid!'

The tube of the vacuum cleaner fell out of Janet's hand and she clutched the banister rail for support. 'Mr Jameson gave you – ?'

'Not Jameson,' said Eddie. 'We went to Gleesons, that big jeweller's in the High Street. The stone was a diamond, with no cracks.'

Janet shook her head, trying to recover her wits. 'Where will you go now?' she asked Slade. 'To a hotel?'

'He'd rather stay here, Mum,' said Eddie hopefully.

'Here?'

'This is only place I know,' said Slade. 'And you are kind people. Will you let me stay with you? I will pay you of course.'

'You see?' said Eddie triumphantly. 'He cottons at last!'

THREE

Slade was a perfect lodger. He left the house each morning after breakfast and didn't come back till early evening. Janet told the neighbours he was an inspector ... of some kind.

First he explored Stanwyck, then he set off for central London, armed with a guide book. His English improved rapidly.

One day Eddie found him in Stanwyck library turning the pages of a history book with barely a glance at each one. Surely no one could read that fast? Slade's cap was pulled down over his forehead. What if it contained a micro-TV transmitter with a lens concealed in the badge?

That night Slade was watching television in the kitchen. Janet had gone to the coffee bar for the evening. Eddie sidled up to the cap which hung on its hook on the hall stand. He put it on his head.

He stood for some time, feeling nothing, hearing nothing. He was about to take the cap off, disappointed, when a voice – a woman's voice – came from inside it.

She was speaking in a strange, lilting language.

After a little while she paused, waiting for a reply, then began again, more urgently. Eddie could guess what she was saying: 'Calling Slade. Do you read me? Answer please. ....'

Hearing Slade moving in the kitchen, Eddie put the cap back on the hook and ran up to his room. He sat on his bed, heart pounding.

Slade *was* a spy! But what kind of spy could be so incapable, so openly innocent? Where on earth did he come from? The bizarre answer came back into Eddie's mind once more ... *nowhere on earth*.

He realised that the television had been switched off and he peeped downstairs. Slade was taking his cap off the hall stand. He often took it to his room at night. So that he could report to his chief? This time his chief would have something to report to him!

Eddie felt a stab of fear. Slade had said he wished no harm to anyone on earth, but what if his mission were threatened? Might his chief order him to take whatever steps were necessary ...?

Footsteps sounded on the stairs.

Eddie ran to the window. It was only a short drop to the roof of the shed in the yard. He put his hands under the sash, but it wouldn't budge.

Then the door opened and Slade came in, looking grim.

'Hi!' said Eddie bravely.

Slade closed the door behind him. 'Have you been playing with my cap?' he demanded.

'I ... I only wanted to try it on ... to see how I

30

looked in it.'

'You heard speaking, yes?'

'Speaking?' Eddie sounded vague. 'I did hear something. Was it Radio One?'

Slade took a step forward and Eddie pressed himself against the wall. This was it! Smash the window? Yell for help?

But Slade spoke gently, pleading not threatening. 'So many years of training, so much planning and hard work, to make my mission possible. All will be ended if you tell people.'

'I won't tell anyone, I promise, straight up! I don't want to spoil things for you, Alf. I want you to stay here!'

Eddie realised that he meant every word. He didn't want Slade's mission to end – the most exciting thing that had ever happened to him in his whole life! But would Slade believe him, trust him?

'Thank you, Eddie. I am most grateful,' Slade said with relief and he went back down the stairs.

Eddie mopped sweat off his brow. Of course Slade trusted him! It was his extraordinary nature to trust anyone . . .

Next morning Slade sat on the bed-settee with the cap on his head and spoke to Control Commander in his own language. 'What are the orders, CC?'

'Mission Directors want you to observe Earth persons at work,' replied Control Commander. 'Item 12 on your Schedule of Operations.'

After breakfast Slade set off down Latimer Road. A milkman was putting bottles on doorsteps and a policeman was strolling by on his beat. Vans and lorries were delivering goods in the High Street. People were going to work in shops and offices.

'There are many different kinds of work to study,' said Slade to CC.

'It might be fruitful if you did work yourself,' suggested CC. 'That way you will learn the procedures at first handle, as the Earth people say.'

'At first hand,' corrected Slade.

He turned into a baker's shop where a manageress and a hard-pressed assistant were serving customers. Slade stepped behind the counter and nodded to the next woman in the queue.

'Six of those currant buns, please,' she said, pointing to a tray.

Slade was picking out the buns when the manageress spotted him. 'Leave those alone!' she said angrily. 'Get out of here at once!'

Further down the street he found men digging a trench in the road. He picked up an unused shovel and jumped into the trench beside them.

'What d'you think you're doing?' demanded the foreman. 'Go away!'

Slade climbed out of the trench wearily. 'People don't want me to work,' he complained.

He turned into Morley Avenue, a street of large old houses. There was a rubbish skip in the roadway outside one of them. The front door was open and there were sounds of men at work inside.

As Slade went up the steps to the front door a small, thin man came out. He wore a toothbrush moustache and a worried look.

'Who are you?' he asked.

'My name is Slade. I wish, please, to work.'

The little man looked pleased. 'Ah, good! Fred promised he'd send someone this morning. My name's Montague. Come in.'

Eddie, who had been following Slade since he left Latimer Road, saw him go into the house and the front door close behind him.

'Had a nice day, Alf?' asked Janet when she gave him his dinner that evening.

'I've been to work,' said Slade with a touch of pride.

'Work?'

'I'm helping to fit out a flat in an old house.'

'What do you know about building?' asked Eddie.

'I watch Mike and Sandy and do what they tell me. Mike is called the chippie. He makes cupboards and things. Sandy is a painter. Mr Montague is the boss. He says we must have the flat finished by Saturday because a dual wish to move in on Monday.' Seeing their blank looks he explained, 'A young man and woman.'

'A *couple*,' said Eddie.

'That's right. They have a baby. On Monday they must leave the room where they are living now and

33

they've nowhere else to go.'

By Saturday night Slade looked glum. 'The flat is not finished,' he reported.

'What a shame,' said Janet.

Slade nodded. 'Mike and Sandy are kind men. They wish to work tomorrow to make it ready. But Mr Montague is kind too. He wants them to have their day off.'

Janet sighed. 'I expect they want to work on Sunday because they get paid more for overtime.'

'And Montague won't fork out the lolly,' added Eddie.

Slade shook his head in disbelief. 'It happens sometimes that people can't agree which is the best way to help others.'

'It's the same at school,' agreed Eddie. 'The teachers want to teach us and we'd rather they took a rest.'

Janet gave him an angry look.

'Since no one has asked me what *I* wish,' said Slade, 'I will try to make things right.'

'How?' asked Eddie.

'I'll go there tomorrow and finish the job myself.'

'You! On your own?'

'There is much work for one man but I shall make – what do you call it? – overtime.'

The next morning Eddie made his way to the house in Morley Avenue.

The front door opened when he gave it a push.

34

Another door led into what was now a ground-floor flat. There was a strong smell of fresh paint and sounds of movement came from a room at the back.

Eddie peeped into the room and blinked.

A figure was darting about like a demented gnat. A streak of white shirt, white slacks and a cap on top confirmed that it was Slade. He ran a strip of wallpaper down one of the walls and smoothed it out in seconds. Then he nipped to a trestle-table to paste another sheet of paper. The brush whisked to and fro in a blur which made Eddie giddy to watch.

After three more trips to the wall Slade began to slow down. He hung the last sheet of paper at normal speed and sat on a packing-case to cool down.

He looked up in surprise when he saw Eddie. 'What are you doing here?'

'I came to see how you're getting on. I'd like to help.'

'Is very kind of you,' said Slade, 'but you can't work as fast as me. Better I carry on alone. Please tell your mother I may not be back till late tonight.'

Eddie retreated into the passage but he was too curious to leave the house. He squinted into the room again.

The camera stood on the window sill. Slade pressed the button and stepped back in front of it. After a few seconds delay there was a faint click and for a brief moment he was bathed in a flash of orange light.

Then he began to move at the same dizzy speed as

before. He snatched up the trestle-table and Eddie jumped aside as it whizzed past him down the passage. In less than a minute Slade was hanging wallpaper again, in a larger room at the front of the house.

Eddie went into the other room, staring in fascination at the camera on the window-sill. Greatly daring, he stretched out a finger, pressed the button, and stepped back in front of it . . .

'The Directors are displeased,' reported CC.

'Oh? What's bugging them?' asked Slade, as he pasted another sheet of wallpaper.

'You're interfering in Earth affairs, contrary to Section 8 of the Manual of Instructions.'

'I'm only getting a flat ready for a young couple who need it.'

'The Directors say you should leave the Earthmen to sort out their own affairs.'

'But the Great Alph tells us we should always help others if we can.'

'Commands of the Great Alph do not apply to Earth persons,' said CC firmly.

'I don't see why not.'

He was putting the paper on the wall when Eddie came briskly into the room. 'Eddie? I thought you'd gone home.'

'Please let me help you, Alf. I can paste the paper while you're hanging it.' Eddie went to the trestle-table and picked up the brush.

'Alert, alert!' hissed CC in Slade's ear. 'The boy's

36

time-curve is the same as yours!'

Slade stared at Eddie. 'You have used the time-curve adjuster!' he said accusingly.

Eddie grinned. 'Now I know what you mean by overtime, Alf. Funny thing is, I don't feel any different. Only the air rushing by every time I move.'

He glanced out of the window as an open sports car went down the street. The driver's hair was being blown out in the wind, yet the car seemed to be travelling no faster than walking pace.

Various uses for Slade's camera began to flash through Eddie's mind. Winning a gold medal at the Olympic Games, just for starters...

Mike and Sandy strolled down Morley Avenue that afternoon on their way home from the pub.

'Pity about that job,' said Mike, shaking his large carroty head.

'I feel sorry for them youngsters with no home to go to tomorrow,' agreed Sandy who became very gloomy after a few beers. 'We'd have got it done today if it wasn't for that tightfisted old –'

He stopped as the front door of the house sprang open and a small figure darted down the steps. It tipped a pile of rubbish into the skip and hurtled back into the house.

'Did you see something, Mike?' asked Sandy after a lengthy pause.

Mike nodded. 'I think I saw something ... or someone ... but it moved so fast I couldn't say....'

'Glad you saw it too,' said Sandy.

Both took a step backwards as the figure sprang into view again.

Eddie ran down the steps, ignoring the two men on the pavement. He tipped another load of rubbish into the skip and returned to the house.

'There's something inside there,' said Sandy thoughtfully. 'We ought to take a look.'

'*You* take a look if you want to.'

Sandy shook his head and they moved on together down the street.

'Did you ever think about giving up booze?' he asked.

'I'm thinking about it right now.'

When Eddie fell into bed that night he felt as if he had worked non-stop for a week. Slade had promised to rouse him early next morning but this proved difficult.

When they reached Morley Avenue Montague was arguing with Mike and Sandy outside the house.

'I tell you I did *not* hire scab labour,' Montague protested.

'Then how did you get the job done?' enquired Mike belligerently.

'I don't know any more about it than you do!'

'I must explain to them,' said Slade, about to go forward.

Eddie put a warning hand on his arm. 'I wouldn't try if I were you.'

Mike closed his big raw fists. 'Just let me get my hands on whoever it was who sneaked in there behind our backs!' he said. 'I'll break their necks for 'em!'

'See what I mean?' said Eddie.

'Why are they angry?' asked Slade.

A young woman came out of the house holding a baby in her arms.

'It's a lovely flat!' she said. 'I want to thank you. You don't know how wonderful it is, to have a real home at last!'

Then her husband came down the steps and tugged at a mattress on top of a handcart heaped with second-hand furniture.

Mike shuffled uncomfortably, then stepped forward. 'Hang about,' he said. 'I'll give you a hand with that.'

They carried the mattress into the house between them.

'You think I should say nothing?' asked Slade.

'Yes, I do,' said Eddie. 'Come on. Let's go now.'

When they reached the corner they looked back. Montague and Sandy were carrying a settee into the house.

'I told you they were kind men,' said Slade, contented.

FOUR

'Do me a favour, Alf.' Eddie laid his school atlas on the kitchen table, open at a map of the stars. 'Show me where you come from. I know so much now you might as well tell me the rest.'

'I come from Alphadelt,' said Slade softly, 'as near as I can call it in your tongue.'

'Is that a planet like Earth?'

'Yes.'

'Then it goes round another star, like our Sun?'

'Yes. But you won't find it on this map.'

'Why not?'

'Because we live in a different time-zone. Here on Earth you can see only what's in your own time-zone, but we can see into others. We can see the Earth, though you can't see Alphadelt. We can even travel from one time-zone to another. We've sent many probes to look at the Earth.'

'Probes?'

'Unmanned spacetime ships. You can't see those either, except when they move into your zero-time, which you call the present.'

'U.F.O.'s!' said Eddie with inspiration. 'Unidentified Flying Objects! People see them appear suddenly, and then disappear.'

'That would be our probes,' agreed Slade, 'moving into your time and out again. One of them picked up things, like these clothes and a camera. They helped us to learn your language and many other things we had to know in order to plan my mission.'

'Are you the first Alph to come to Earth?'

Slade nodded. 'I had just arrived when you found me in the park.'

'How come I didn't see you land?'

'I was still a few minutes behind Earth-zero when I came down among the trees and stowed my ship away.'

'Stowed it away?'

'By compaction.'

Eddie studied him. 'You look just like us. Why aren't you different, coming from a different planet?'

'We are,' said Slade, 'but we've learnt how to mould living tissue into different shapes. Our surgeons changed my body to make me look like an Earthman.'

'They did a good job.'

'They had a model to work from. Some time ago you lost two astronauts when their ship went out of orbit. A man and a woman. We were too late to save them but we were able to examine their bodies.'

'You've gone to an awful lot of trouble to get here,' said Eddie.

'Is is not worth it, to study life on another planet?

My mission is called Spacetime Link, Attitude and Destination Earth.'

'Spacetime Link. S . . . L . . .' Eddie grinned. 'Now I get it. S.L.A.D.E!'

It was Saturday afternoon. Eddie was strolling down the High Street with Jimmy and Gas.

'Hey, Eddie,' said Jimmy, 'there's your lodger.'

He pointed to a street corner where Slade was talking to a small, elderly woman with silvery hair. She held a box in her hand, collecting money for charity.

'He's foreign, isn't he?' said Gas. 'Where does he come from?'

'And what's he doing here?' added Jimmy.

It wasn't the first time they had asked questions about Slade and Eddie decided to shut them up. 'If you must know, he came in a flying saucer to take a look at the Earth.'

The reaction was what he expected.

'Ha, ha, very funny!' said Jimmy sourly. 'I bet he's some kind of crook.'

'That's more like it,' agreed Gas.

A heavily-built man wearing a striped suit and a Panama hat dropped a coin in the collecting box, raising his hat to the old lady as she thanked him. Slade moved off down the street.

Eddie didn't see him again till dinner time, when he was very thoughtful.

'The more I see of your people the more confused I

become,' he said.

'Why is that?' asked Janet as she put his plate in front of him.

'With one hand they take all they can, with the other they give with much kindness.'

'People were collecting money for the Children's Fund this afternoon,' Eddie explained.

'I spoke to one of them,' said Slade. 'Her name is Mrs Hart. She's the treasurer of the local committee. I said I was making reports of such things and she promised to tell me more about it. I will go to see her this evening. Where is Alderney Avenue?'

'It's off Miller Street,' said Janet. 'Nice part of town. Eddie will take you there.'

Eddie glared at his mother. 'Why me?'

'To show how kind you are,' said Janet sweetly.

Eddie and Slade went up a path to the front door of Number 7 Alderney Avenue, a large house standing in its own grounds.

Mrs Hart answered the doorbell. 'So nice of you to come,' she said, smiling.

'This is Eddie, a friend of mine,' said Slade.

'I'm pleased to meet you,' said Mrs Hart. 'Do come in.'

They stepped into an oak-panelled hall.

'You have a nice home,' said Slade.

'Too big for me now I live here alone,' sighed Mrs Hart. 'Tell me, which newspaper do you represent?'

'*The Stanwyck Gazette*,' said Eddie, knowing that

43

Slade found it difficult to tell a lie even for the sake of his mission.

Mrs Hart glanced at the camera over Slade's shoulder and put a hand to her hair. 'Are you going to take a picture?' she asked.

'Not just yet,' said Slade. 'Please tell me about your collecting.'

'We've had a very successful day. I'll show you the figures.'

They followed her into a drawing-room full of elegant period furniture. A row of collecting boxes stood on a table. Mrs Hart went to a bureau and showed them a sheet of paper containing a neat list of names with figures entered beside them. The total at the bottom was £732.46.

'It's the most we've ever collected in a single day,' she said proudly. 'It means so much to the children in need. I shall take the money to the bank on Monday and send a cheque to...'

She stopped suddenly, staring at the table. 'Where is it? Where's the money?'

'In the boxes?' asked Eddie.

'No, they're empty. I counted it out and put it into bags. They've gone!'

'How is that possible?' asked Slade.

'Anyone else been in here?' enquired Eddie.

'I told you, I live alone.'

'Could anyone get into the house?'

'I've been having my dinner. I didn't hear...' She stopped again. 'Oh, look! The window! I only opened it a little, to let in some air.'

Eddie strode to the window which was open wide. It didn't need Sherlock Holmes to detect the traces of garden dirt on the sill.

'Someone got in through here,' he announced. 'Must have been a thief. Someone who takes what doesn't belong to him,' he added for Slade's benefit.

'Oh, my goodness!' Mrs Hart's voice trembled and she fell into a chair.

'They give and they take,' said Slade, shaking his head.

'What will the committee think?' moaned Mrs Hart. 'They're sure to blame me! I must call the police at once.' But she was too overcome even to stand up.

'I'll call them, shall I?' said Eddie.

'No need to make fuss,' said Slade, suddenly in command. 'Better to ask this thief to give the money back, then no one will be hurt.'

They both stared at him, puzzled.

'Do you know who it is?' asked Mrs Hart.

'Not yet, but I will soon find out. Do not trouble yourself about the money, Mrs Hart. I promise I will bring it back to you tonight.'

Mrs Hart stared at him and seemed to trust him instinctively. 'I'll wait for you,' she said gratefully.

'How are you going to find the thief?' asked Eddie as he followed Slade from the house.

Slade stopped outside the gate. 'I found *you*, didn't

I, when you took my bag from the bus shelter?' He raised his camera to his eye, peering through the viewfinder and twisting the focus control.

'What are you doing with that?'

'I'm looking back in time. Ah! I can see someone in the garden.'

Eddie stared at the garden. 'There's no one here.'

'Not now. In the past.' Slade took the camera from his eye to glance at the dial. 'About fifteen minutes ago. If you don't believe me, look for yourself.' He handed the camera to Eddie. 'Keep turning that slowly,' he said, pointing to the focus control.

Eddie put the camera to his eye, twisting the control, and gave a gasp of astonishment. A big man wearing a striped suit and a Panama hat was in Mrs Hart's garden. It was the man who had strolled down the High Street that afternoon. Now he wore gloves, and the pockets of his thin summer jacket bulged and sagged with the weight of banknotes and coins. He was facing the road, moving rapidly towards the house *in reverse*.

'He's going backwards!' said Eddie.

Slade nodded. 'That's because you're moving the time-scanner further back.'

The man disappeared backwards through the window into the drawing-room.

'He's inside now,' reported Eddie.

'No need to go back any further,' said Slade. 'Stop turning the control and keep watching. You'll see past time moving forward again at its usual speed.'

Keeping his eye to the viewfinder, Eddie saw the man appear at the window again from inside. Moving forwards at a normal rate, he climbed through the window and hurried across the garden. Suddenly he ducked behind the hedge.

'He's stopped,' reported Eddie. 'He's keeping out of sight.'

'Someone coming down the road, perhaps?' suggested Slade.

Eddie moved the camera round. A tall man in a yachting outfit and a rather scruffy boy were coming towards the gate. Eddie gasped again. 'It's us! He was there when we arrived!'

Eddie watched himself and Slade go up to the house. Mrs Hart opened the door and let him in. Eddie turned the camera round again. The man in the striped suit rose from behind the hedge, hurried out of the gate and made off down the road.

'He's going, that way . . .' Eddie pointed.

'All we have to do now is keep him in view and follow him,' said Slade.

After Sam Jefferson made his escape from Alderney Avenue he headed for the railway station looking forward to a well-earned holiday. Once the money had been spent he could return to Stanwyck. There would be no evidence against him.

He bought a ticket for central London and climbed the steps to the platform on the railway viaduct. Having twenty minutes to wait for a train, he moved to the far end of the platform where he was not likely to be noticed. The bags of money made his body bulge even more than usual.

Ten minutes later a man in yachting gear came up the steps with a boy beside him. With a shock Sam recognised the two visitors to Number 7 Alderney Avenue. What were they doing here? The boy pointed and both strode towards him.

Sam turned in panic and took the only way of escape open to him ... down the ramp at the end of the platform and along the railway track. A goods train was rumbling slowly towards him on the other line.

He had not travelled more than a few yards when a purple haze shone in front of his eyes. A moment later it was gone, but in that moment an extraordinary thing happened. The goods train took flight! Suddenly it was hurtling along at the speed of an intercity express, its monotonous clanking changed to a furious rattle. He shuddered as it sped past him.

Next, to his horror, the man and the boy came into view, one either side of him. Only they weren't running like he was. They were strolling comfortably. Sam was dimly aware that in some crazy fashion he must be travelling very slowly while everything else went on at normal speed.

He forced his heavy body to move faster and sweat poured down his cheeks. The other two merely increased their pace a fraction to keep up with him.

'Take the money, Alf,' said Eddie.

'I prefer that he should give it to me,' said Slade.

Their voices reached Sam's ears as a high-pitched gabble like a tape played too fast.

Then Slade spoke slowly, drawing out each syllable, so that Sam could take it in. 'You have taken money which does not belong to you. It belongs to children who need it badly. Please give it back.'

Sam was gasping for breath and his legs were growing weak. Was he mad? Or dreaming? He remembered childhood nightmares of long ago ... running, running ... unable to escape ...

'I wish only that you do what is right,' Slade explained patiently.

At that moment Sam's foot missed a sleeper and he tripped over the next one. As he pitched forwards he heard a sharp 'peep-peep' in the distance and wondered vaguely what it was.

Eddie, who heard the two-tone horn at its proper pitch, knew all too well what it was. 'Train coming, Alf!' he warned.

The express from Dover was pounding through Stanwyck Station at nearly eighty miles an hour.

Sam floated downwards like a descending balloon till he landed flat on his face in the middle of the track.

Slade bent over him, grabbed him under the armpits and heaved. But strong as he was he could not lift Sam's body, trapped in its slower time-curve, at more than a snail's pace.

'Quick!' yelled Eddie in panic. He grabbed Sam's legs and heaved too, but it was like trying to shift a ten-ton weight.

'We can't do it!' cried Eddie.

But even as he spoke, the effect of the time-dose began to ease and Sam's body yielded.

As the roar of the train grew louder in their ears and the track shuddered under their feet, they heaved him sideways ... and both fell beside him in the narrow space between the railway tracks. Then the train filled the night with lightning flashes from its windows and a storm of thunder from its wheels, only inches away.

After what seemed an age, it was gone and the viaduct stopped shaking. Slade and Eddie stood up.

'Am I awake?' muttered Sam fearfully, raising his head.

'You're awake,' said Eddie. 'Are you going to hand over the loot now or do we push you under the next train?'

'Eddie!' said Slade sternly. 'You must not threaten.'

Sam put a pudgy hand into one pocket and then another, hauling out the bags of money.

'Take it,' he said. 'Take it and get me out of here!'

'I can't tell you how grateful I am,' said Mrs Hart, her eyes moist with tears. 'How did you persuade him to give it back?'

'It wasn't difficult,' said Eddie. 'We just took our time.'

FIVE

Eddie came downstairs. 'Morning, CC,' he said brightly to the cap on the hall stand.

Slade was reading a newspaper in the kitchen. 'Please can you explain something I don't understand,' he said.

'Maybe,' said Eddie, wondering what was coming this time.

'What is war?'

Eddie sat at the table and helped himself to cornflakes. 'When people can't get what they want any other way they start shooting each other.'

Slade frowned. 'Please don't make jokes. I wish to know the truth.'

'Who's joking?' said Eddie. 'Haven't you heard of the H-bomb?'

'What is that?'

Slade listened to Eddie's explanation with incredulous horror.

'If ever they start dropping them it'll be over in four minutes flat,' Eddie concluded. 'And don't bother to make a will. There won't be anyone left.'

Slade spoke faintly. 'What's to stop someone

dropping one right now?'

'Nothing,' admitted Eddie, 'except they're afraid we'll do the same to them. Let's hope no one is that crazy.'

Slade rose unsteadily and went out of the room. He took his cap into the front room and closed the door. 'Calling Control,' he said.

'CC here,' replied the calm voice.

Slade spoke urgently for several minutes.

'This is a grave matter,' admitted CC. 'I'll report it to the Mission Directors at once.'

'Tell them I want to leave this planet right away.'

'Leave?' said CC, astonished.

'If my life depends on Earth people behaving sensibly, the risk is too great. I could be wiped out with the rest of them in four minutes!'

'I understand that,' said Control patiently, 'but if you are so worried, use your time-scanner. Look ahead.'

Slade took the camera to the window and peered at Latimer Road through the viewfinder. He twisted the focus control further and further till the scene became fuzzy.

'I'm looking as far as the time horizon,' he reported. 'The street is still there.'

'I thought as much,' said Control. 'You're in no immediate danger.'

Slade put the camera back on the sideboard and opened the door. Eddie, crouching at the keyhole, sprang back guiltily.

'You have been listening again!' said Slade.

Eddie nodded sheepishly. 'You're not going to leave, are you, Alf?'

'No.'

Eddie smiled and pointed to the camera. 'Can you really look ahead through that, as well as backwards?'

'Of course. It depends which way you twist the scanning control.'

Eddie stared at the camera thoughtfully. 'If you can see things that are going to happen ... does that mean you can't stop them happening?'

'No, it doesn't,' said Slade. 'What's past can't be changed, of course, but what's to come is not certain. The scanner can only see existing time-curves projected into the future. If someone interferes, the direction of a curve may be changed and then the future will be different.'

Ideas scampered through Eddie's brain like playful hares. He sorted out one of them for immediate attention.

'Have you studied sport yet?'

'Not yet. It's a good idea. Which should I start with?'

'Horse racing,' said Eddie promptly. 'And I'll help you.'

The sun was shining warmly on the racecourse when Eddie and Slade arrived in time to see the first race begin.

'They're off!' shouted the crowd as the starting-gate rose and the horses galloped away, jockeys perched high on their backs, heads low, urging them on. Soon they disappeared round the first bend.

'Where are they going?' asked Slade.

'To the winning-post, of course.'

'Where is that?'

'Right there, in front of us.'

'But this is where they started from.'

'They're racing,' explained Eddie patiently. 'Whichever gets back first is the winner. Don't you have races on Alphadelt?'

'People enjoy running fast,' agreed Slade, 'but if you're ahead of someone else it's only polite to slow down and let him catch up.'

When the horses were parading for the second race Eddie spoke casually, 'Take a look ahead, Alf. Which of these is going to win?'

'Why do you wish to know?'

'Just to see how the scanner works.'

'Oh, very well.' Slade raised the camera, pointed it at the winning-post and turned the control. 'The rider in the blue and white shirt. Number 7.'

'Ta,' said Eddie. 'Scuse me. Shan't be long.' He hurried off, disappearing among the crowds.

He was back again before the race began. Number 7 started off in the middle of the bunch and, when the horses reached the far side of the course, was well behind the leaders.

'He's a long way back,' said Eddie, worried. 'Are

you sure you got it right?'

'Does it matter?'

'Oh no, not at all.'

Nearing the last bend, Number 7 began to move up, passing one horse after another. It reached the final straight in third place.

'Come on, Hangman's Creek!' yelled Eddie.

As if in answer Hangman's Creek put on another burst of speed. It overtook the horse in second place and, with a furlong to go, moved abreast of the leader. It passed the winning-post half a length in front.

'He's won!' screamed Eddie.

'I said he would,' said Slade, puzzled.

After a pause to get his breath back Eddie said, 'Take a gander at the next race. Which is going to win that?'

Slade hesitated, but raised the camera. 'Number 14.'

'Wait for me.' Eddie dashed off into the crowd again.

'That boy is up to something,' said CC in Slade's ear. 'I think you should find out what it is.'

Number 14 romped home with several lengths to spare to Eddie's great delight. 'Now the next one,' he said.

'I don't wish to look any more,' said Slade.

'Please, Alf. Just once more.'

Slade raised the camera for the third time. 'Number 5.'

'Great! Stay there.'

Eddie ran off and this time Slade followed him, almost losing him among the crowds. He found him talking to a bookmaker, who stood on a platform with a blackboard behind him, marked with the runners of the next race.

The bookmaker was counting out ten pound notes.

'Put it all on Sharp Corner, Number 5,' said Eddie.

'The whole lot?'

'Yes.'

'Where d'you get your tips?' enquired the bookie.

'Got second sight, haven't I?' said Eddie, grinning as he set off back to the stand.

Slade turned to a racegoer beside him. 'Tell me please, what is this man doing here?'

'Doing?' The racegoer looked oddly at Slade. 'He's a bookmaker.'

'You mean, an author?'

The man laughed. 'You're a right one! Bookies take bets on the races. You put your money on a horse, right? If it loses, the bookie keeps your money. If it wins, he pays you back plus the odds.'

'So that's what it's all about!' said CC in Slade's ear. 'We might have known!'

There was no sign of the familiar yachting cap and the blue jacket on the stand. Nor was there time to search for Slade. The horses were at the starting-line. A moment later they were off.

Sharp Corner was well up among the leaders. In the back straight he was lying in second place. When the horses rounded the bend in the final straight, Eddie was jumping up and down with joy. Sharp Corner was two lengths ahead of the rest.

And that's when the time-curves began to go haywire. Eddie was possibly the only person in the crowd to notice the purple flash – only a very faint one – that illuminated Sharp Corner. Immediately, the horse's pace slackened. His jockey, startled, flicked him with the crop but it had no effect. The next horse was overtaking when a second flash slowed him down, too, and they plunged on, neck and neck, with the rest catching up.

A faint orange glow appeared around several slower horses, coming round the bend at the back of the field, and they showed remarkable bursts of speed, quickly catching up with the leaders.

After that the flashes were fired at rapid intervals, slowing one horse, speeding up another.

Eddie spotted Slade, standing by the rail opposite the winning post. 'Stop, Alf!' he yelled.

His voice was drowned in the startled roar that arose from the crowd. The horses were closing up till they were strung out across the course side by side.

It was a finish never before known in racing history – an entire field passing the winning-post in a straight line.

After the judges had agonised over the photographs they named twelve winners but Sharp Corner was not one of them.

*   *   *

Eddie went to his room early that night to nurse his grievance and when he came downstairs next morning Slade had left the house.

'D'you know where he's gone?' asked Eddie.

'To the library, I think,' said Janet. 'He said he wants to look up books on gambling.'

Eddie peeped into the front room. The camera lay on the sideboard.

Thanks to Slade's interference at the racecourse, Eddie knew he would need some sort of protection that day. Why shouldn't Slade provide it? The camera, in its curious way, was a powerful weapon. Eddie slung it over his shoulder and went out.

He was crossing the wasteland by the railway viaduct when Jimmy's voice called, 'Hi!' Eddie turned quickly in the opposite direction, but Gas was coming that way. They had him trapped.

'Hi, fellas,' he said, trying to strike a cheerful note. 'Nice day, isn't it?'

But they weren't interested in the weather.

'Where's my money?' asked Jimmy.

'And mine,' said Gas.

There was no dodging the issue. 'Things didn't go quite like I planned,' Eddie confessed. 'There's no need to get stroppy. It wasn't my fault.'

'You borrowed a fiver from both of us,' Jimmy reminded him. 'You said you'd give us back ten each after the races.'

'You said you couldn't lose,' added Gas.

'I won the first two races. I was going to clean up

on the third when ... when things went wrong.'

'I want my tenner,' said Jimmy, curling his brawny fists.

'Me too,' said Gas, his pudgy face unusually determined.

Eddie raised the camera to his eye, finger on the focus control. 'Ten quid each isn't much,' he mused. 'Wouldn't you like to double it?'

'How?' asked Gas.

'Have a bet with me.'

'What sort of bet?'

'Anything.' Eddie lowered the camera. 'For instance, I bet you that the next car to come round the corner over there is a Rover. A white Rover, $3\frac{1}{2}$-litre.'

'How can you bet on a thing like that?' asked Gas. 'There's thousands of cars it might be.'

'It's my hard cheddar if I'm wrong. Double or quits. What d'you say?'

'I'll bet you it's some other car,' said Gas promptly.

They had only a few moments to wait before a white $3\frac{1}{2}$-litre Rover came round the corner.

'I don't believe it!' said Gas.

'We're quits,' said Eddie, raising the camera again. 'How about you, Jimmy?'

Jimmy shook his head. 'I'm not making bets with someone who can guess like that.'

'There's no time to argue about it,' said Eddie. 'I reckon your dad's looking for you, and he's pretty 'angry too.'

'He can't be. He's gone to do a job in Croydon. He won't be back till tonight.'

'I bet you he's still here. If I'm wrong I owe you twenty quid. If I'm right we're all square. Fair enough?'

'Done!' said Jimmy. 'You owe me twenty quid.'

'Jimmy!' called an angry voice.

Jimmy swung round, his face suddenly pale. 'Dad!'

'What the —— have you done with my drill?' demanded his father. 'Hilda says you had it last night. You know I can't work without it!'

'Coming, Dad,' said Jimmy, hurrying away.

'We're quits!' Eddie called after him.

'How did you *know*?' asked Gas, incredulous.

'Let this be a lesson to you,' said Eddie smugly. 'Never gamble!'

Eddie mooched around town on his own, taking glimpses through the scanner into past and future. All he could see was people going about their daily business.

He paused when he saw a man with a white stick standing on a corner in the High Street. A tray containing cheap digital watches hung round his neck. In spite of his dark glasses, the man was glancing up and down the street. Then he took what looked like a walkie-talkie from his pocket and spoke into it.

Curious, Eddie raised the camera to his eye. Traffic and people in the street whipped by at high

60

speed as he pushed the time control into the future . . .
until he saw a security van approaching through the
busy traffic. Then he stopped moving the control and
let future time unfold at its natural pace.

The watchseller pulled out his walkie-talkie again
and spoke into it urgently. A few moments later the
security van stopped outside a bank. The driver got
out, looked around him and nodded to a second man
who stepped out of the van with a black case strapped
to his wrist.

As they strode into the bank, a yellow Ford Cortina
drove up at speed and stopped in front of the van.
One man stayed at the wheel. Two others jumped out
wearing stockings over their faces. The watchseller
chucked his tray and stick on to the pavement and
joined them. All three dived into the bank and the
door closed behind them.

Eddie kept his eye glued to the viewfinder, keenly
aware that he could not stop what was happening
since it *wasn't* happening – yet.

A few minutes later, future time, the three men
came running from the bank, one of them holding the
security case, and piled into the Cortina which drove
off at high speed . . .

SIX

Readers in the Public Library looked up startled as Eddie hurried in. Slade was turning the pages of a book.

'Alf!' called Eddie in a hoarse whisper.

Slade noticed the camera slung over Eddie's shoulder. 'What are you doing with that?' he demanded.

Eddie handed it to Slade. 'I only borrowed it, for a bit of fun. But I saw something happening, in the future.'

There were sharp looks from other people and Slade led Eddie to the entrance hall. 'What did you see?' he asked.

'There's going to be a bank raid in the High Street.' Eddie described carefully everything he had seen through the time-scanner.

'Was anyone hurt?' was Slade's first question.

'There might have been, inside the bank.'

'Have you told anyone else?'

'How can I? They'll ask how I know.'

'How long before it happens?'

Eddie pointed to the camera. 'According to the

dial, about twenty-five minutes, but it's taken me five minutes to get here.'

'I must go to the bank and warn them,' decided Slade.

'You are making another interference in Earth affairs,' warned CC as Slade turned into the High Street with Eddie at his heels. 'The Directors will be most displeased.'

'Someone might be hurt if I don't prevent it,' muttered Slade doggedly.

The watchseller was standing on the street corner near the bank just as Eddie had described.

'You must stay out of this, Eddie,' said Slade. 'Go back home and wait for me.' He strode into the bank alone.

A customer was sitting at a table filling in a form. Another was handing money over the counter to a clerk. Slade approached a second clerk and spoke quietly, anxious not to cause any panic. 'There's going to be a raid on this bank in less than ten minutes,' he said.

The girl merely raised an eyebrow. He might have been querying an entry in his account. 'I'll inform the manager,' she said.

Slade waited impatiently while she went to an office at the back. She returned with the manager, who came through the door in the security screen.

'Is there something I can do for you, sir?' he asked politely.

Slade spoke quietly but urgently. 'Lock the doors at once and call the coppermen, I mean the police. Three men are coming here in a few minutes to raid the bank.'

The manager's smooth manner was unruffled. He had dealt with too many cranks and conmen to be easily fooled. 'What makes you think that, sir?'

Slade paused and his hesitation confirmed the manager's suspicions. 'Did the robbers send you here to warn us?' he enquired sarcastically.

'I have information,' said Slade. 'You must believe me. Look.'

Slade led the manager to the doorway and pointed to the watchseller on the street corner. 'That man is not blind. He's one of the gang.'

The manager smiled indulgently. 'I doubt it, sir. He's been standing there every day for the past three weeks.'

'Perhaps he's been there to souse out the bank.'

'Souse out – ? Ah! You mean, suss out. That's an ingenious thought,' admitted the manager. 'But we can't make a fouse, I mean, a fuss, on mere suspicion, can we? If you'd care to reveal the source of your information ...?'

The security van was coming down the street towards them.

'You'll be sorry you didn't listen to me!' said Slade angrily. He strode back into the bank and raised his voice. 'Please take care, everyone. Thieves are about to raid the bank!'

At last his words had some effect. The customer at the table looked up startled and the woman at the counter gave a sharp cry of fear.

'Be quiet!' hissed the manager, hurrying after Slade. 'How dare you frighten our staff and customers!' He raised his voice too. 'A false alarm I assure you.'

Several voices spoke at once. Then the two security-men marched in and the girl behind the counter dutifully opened the door in the screen so that they could pass through it.

'Watch out!' warned Slade over the rest.

'Will you shut up!' insisted the manager. 'I assure everyone there is no need for –'

He was interrupted by the woman at the counter who screamed and pointed. The manager swung round.

Two men stood in the doorway with stockings over their faces. One of them, stocky and heavily-built, was holding a gun. The watchseller, still in his dark glasses, came in behind them and closed the door.

The security-men stood stock still and the two frightened customers backed into a corner.

The stocky man pointed his gun at the manager's head and spoke with a strong Cockney accent. 'Hand over the money, you two, or this guy gets done.'

The manager let out a yelp of terror.

The security-men nodded to one another with professional calm. One of them unlocked the black case from the other's wrist.

Then the watchseller hissed a warning. 'Watch out, Carl! That bloke's got a camera!'

Carl, the stocky man, turned his head to see Slade's camera pointing at him. He ducked instantly and a purple ray shot over his head. A fly on the wall, which had been buzzing busily, began to move like an elderly sparrow.

The third member of the gang, taller than the others, moved fast, snatching the camera out of Slade's hand.

Carl straightened up, pointing the gun at Slade. 'Over there!' he ordered angrily.

'Do as he says!' hissed CC in Slade's ear.

Slade moved obediently into the corner beside the two customers.

Eddie had no intention of going home and missing all the excitement. He kept watch on the bank, expecting to see a cop car hurtle into view at any moment. After several minutes none appeared and he looked anxiously at his watch. Surely it was time?

The security van came down the street and the watchseller spoke rapidly into his walkie-talkie. The van drew up and the security men went into the bank. Then, as Eddie watched helplessly, the yellow saloon arrived and two of the men inside it ran into the bank with the watchseller close behind them.

Still there was no police car.

Desperate to know what was happening, Eddie edged up to the bank and raised himself on tiptoe to look through one of the windows.

He saw a security man handing the black case to the stocky bank robber.

Eddie swung round, about to yell for help – and came face to face with the driver of the getaway car. It was a thin, mournful face, heavily scarred. As Eddie opened his mouth, the man clamped a gloved hand over it, grabbed the collar of Eddie's jacket and dragged him across the pavement to the car. He opened the rear door and threw Eddie inside just as the robbers came running from the bank.

The tall man came first with Slade's camera slung over his shoulder. The driver yelled to him, 'Grab that kid, Snowy!'

Eddie was reaching for the handle of the door on the other side of the car when Snowy hauled him back.

The driver jumped in and gunned the engine. The watchseller dived into the back after Snowy. Carl, clutching the black case, threw himself into the front passenger seat as the car zoomed away from the pavement.

It was all happening as Eddie had seen it earlier, except for the extra passenger in the car – himself. He twisted round to look out of the rear window and saw Slade outside the bank staring after the car.

'Sit still!' ordered Snowy, pulling him back into his seat.

'Faster, Les,' muttered Carl. His accent was no longer Cockney but upper class with a slight drawl.

'Doing my best,' grumbled the driver, yanking at the wheel to pass a big lorry.

Carl looked over his shoulder. 'What is this young man doing here?' he asked.

'Caught him looking in through the window of the bank,' said Les, twisting the wheel sharply to turn down a side street. 'He was going to yell so I grabbed him. He saw my face. Couldn't let him go after that, could I?'

'Why didn't you do him in?' asked the watchseller nervously. He was a small, wiry man with red hair.

'Cool it, Spike,' said Snowy calmly.

'We don't want to be stuck with him!' insisted Spike.

'He stays with us for the present,' decided Carl, who was clearly the leader of the gang. 'Blindfold him, Snowy.'

Snowy pulled the stocking off his head to reveal an ebony-black face. He wrapped the stocking round Eddie's eyes and tied it tightly.

Slade saw Eddie's face peering at him from the back of the Cortina and ran after the car with long, powerful strides. He heard the distant siren of a police car approaching the bank, too late!

The Cortina turned down a side street and when Slade rounded the corner, it was far down the street turning once more, to the left.

He found it abandoned at the end of a narrow alley There was no sign of Eddie or the gang and he guessed that the robbers might have had a second car waiting for them.

He ran to the end of the alley and peered down the next street but there was nothing to be seen. There was a high wall on one side of the alley and the back of an office block on the other. He hammered on a door but there was no answer.

Slade was on his way back to the High Street when a police car pulled up beside him.

'Bloke in a yachting outfit,' said the driver. 'This must be him.' He jumped out of the car. 'Excuse me, sir. We want a word with you.'

'I *warned* you not to interfere!' said CC.

Eddie tried to make a mental map of where they were going, but he soon lost track. He didn't even know what car he was travelling in after being bundled blindfold out of one into another.

At last the car stopped and once more he was dragged out by Snowy, who led him across the pavement into a building. The men's boots drummed on bare boards and there was a musty, dusty smell of a place long empty.

They climbed a long flight of creaky wooden stairs and went into a room at the top. The door closed behind them and Snowy took the stocking from Eddie's eyes.

It was a big room with three tall windows covered with wooden planks on the outside. Strips of sunlight coming through the gaps traced a pattern of prison bars on the dusty floorboards. There were a rickety table and chairs, four old beds, a camping stove and a couple of kerosene lamps.

Only Snowy and Spike were still with him.

'Don't try anything stupid,' said Snowy, placing Slade's camera on the mantelpiece.

'He'll have to go,' said Spike. His eyes, no longer hidden by the dark glasses, were small and malevolent.

'Meaning we turn him loose?' enquired Snowy.

Spike spat on the boards. 'I mean dump him in the canal tonight along with a few bricks.'

Eddie felt a knot forming in his stomach.

'You can't do that,' said Snowy quietly. 'He's only a kid.'

Eddie glanced at the black man thankfully.

Carl came into the room. His face was square with a large nose and a determined jaw.

'Where've you hidden the loot?' demanded Spike.

'Where no one will find it,' said Carl. 'It will remain there, out of harm's way, until it's safe for us to leave this place. I warned you we may be here a couple of weeks at least.'

'Why can't we share it out now?'

Carl sighed. 'If you have it now, my dear Spike, you will be tempted to do a bunk. You'd throw tenners around like confetti, showing off to your friends and it wouldn't take a dumb cop five minutes to lay his hands on you. We shall not repeat the mistakes others have made in our position.'

Eddie was inching across the room trying to reach the camera on the mantelpiece. Spike swung round, pointing at him.

'What about him?'

'Ah, yes!' said Carl. 'You're very welcome, young man.'

'Welcome!' gasped Spike.

'Should our good friends on the other side of the law stumble across our hideout by some mischance, this boy could be our passport to freedom.'

'What's that mean?' asked Spike.

'It means Carl wants to keep him as a hostage,' said Snowy.

'What sharp men I have about me,' said Carl admiringly. 'One of us must be responsible for his safety.'

'I'll look after him,' said Snowy.

Footsteps sounded in the hallway below. Carl took out his gun and went on to a landing, looking down the stairs.

'It's Les,' he said, relaxing.

Les, the car driver, came into the room, his face as mournful as ever. 'I've dumped the car,' he said. 'What now?'

'A pleasant evening in each other's company,' suggested Carl.

SEVEN

'How did you know that the man outside the bank was one of the gang?' enquired Inspector Rowse.

'I keep telling you,' said Slade patiently. 'He wasn't blind and he had a walkie-talkie.'

'And that was enough to inform you exactly when and where a raid would take place?'

Slade did not answer. He was weary of the boxlike interrogation room with its square table, hard chairs and relentless questions.

'I must assume, Mr Slade, that you have information which you are concealing. Who are you trying to protect? The boy?'

'Eddie's got nothing to do with the gang.' Slade leaned forward. 'You've got to find him.'

'We have every available man looking for him,' said Rowse calmly. 'You're a stranger to this country, Mr Slade. Where do you come from?'

'I can't tell you,' said Slade.

Rowse raised an eyebrow. 'Do you realise you're committing an offence by refusing to answer my questions? Let me see your passport.'

'What is a passport?'

'I see there are several angles to investigate in this case,' said Rowse thoughtfully.

When Slade left the police station that night he found himself surrounded by newspaper reporters, TV cameras and bombarded with more questions.

'How did you know there was going to be a raid? What did you say to the bank manager? Tell us about yourself, Mr Slade...'

Slade shook his head helplessly and pushed his way through them only to find another group waiting outside Number 22 Latimer Road. He struggled to get through the door and had to push it to keep it shut.

Janet was in the kitchen, her eyes red-rimmed. She turned to him with some relief. 'They've let you go at last? I'm so glad.'

'Inspector Rowse said I could come home tonight, but I mustn't leave the district and I must report to the copperhouse tomorrow.'

'Have they heard anything about Eddie?'

'No, nothing.' He sat down, very tired.

Janet filled the kettle automatically. 'How *did* you know there was going to be a robbery, Alf? And why was Eddie there too?'

'Please, Janet ... I can't explain.'

'What have you told the police?'

'I couldn't tell them either. I'm afraid Inspector Rowse is angry with me. He's going to report me to the . . . the office at home . . .'

'The Home Office?'

'He thinks I may be an illegal immigrate.'

'Immigrant.'

'Is that bad?'

Janet nodded anxiously. 'He can put you in prison.' She sat facing him. 'Alf, you must escape while you can. Go back where you came from. You can do that, can't you, any time you want to?'

'How do you know?'

'Because I'm not such a fool as you think. I can guess, at least I think I can, what you are really doing here.'

'I can't run away now,' said Slade slowly. 'Not until Eddie is safe. If the police can't find him I must look for him myself.'

'But the police may arrest you.'

He looked at her steadily. 'With your help perhaps I can keep out of their way.'

'I'll help you every way I can,' said Janet. 'Please find him, Alf. *Please* . . .'

'The Directors have given instructions,' declared CC when Slade was alone in his room that night. 'Your mission is terminated. You must return to Alphadelt at once.'

'I can't. Not yet.'

'Because of that wretched boy? He's not important.'

'He *is* important,' said Slade, determined. 'Let me

do what is right and proper in the name of the Great Alph.'

'You have your orders!' said CC stiffly. 'Message over.'

Slade hurled the cap on to a chair in disgust and threw himself back on to the bed.

Next morning Janet came home with a parcel under her arm.

Slade was waiting for her anxiously. She untied the parcel to reveal a sports jacket and trousers, shirts, pairs of socks, a floppy cap with a large peak, and a small holdall.

'I hope these will fit you,' she said.

When Slade had changed into his new clothes he took his wad of money from the lining of his yachting jacket and stuffed it in the new sports jacket.

He opened a slit inside the yachting cap and extracted a tiny audio-unit. He found a small pill bottle in the sideboard and put the audio-unit inside it for safety. Then he packed the holdall with the few things he needed.

Ten minutes later, with the floppy cap pulled well down over his eyes, he left Number 22 Latimer Road through the back yard and down the narrow alleyway at the rear of the house.

'Somewhere I want to go,' said Eddie when he woke up the next morning. He was lying on an old mattress in a corner of the big room.

Snowy nodded and swung his lanky frame off a

camp bed. He unfastened the cords round Eddie's wrists and ankles. 'Don't try anything,' he warned.

Eddie marched down the room beside Snowy. Spike and Les lay on beds either side of the fireplace. The camera still stood on the mantelpiece.

'Do you have to untie his hands?' enquired Carl. He sat on a bed beside the door, constantly on guard.

'How would he manage with them tied?' asked Snowy. Of the three men he was the least in awe of Carl.

Eddie followed Snowy out of the room, along the landing, past the head of the L-shaped staircase and into a narrow passage.

'I'll be waiting,' said Snowy.

The lavatory contained a small window with a convenient drainpipe outside but the window was stuck fast and Eddie soon gave up his attempts to open it.

When Eddie and Snowy returned to the big room Les was preparing a breakfast of toast and beans on a camp stove. Snowy brought a plateful for Eddie and another for himself.

'Thanks for looking after me,' said Eddie, quietly so the others wouldn't hear.

'I've got a kid of my own, younger than you.'

'What's your proper name?'

'Sid.'

'Why do they call you Snowy?'

'They think it's witty,' said Snowy.

'How did you get into this game?'

'If you must know, I want my son to have a better start than I did so one day he can go wherever he wants, right to the top if he's clever.'

'Is that why you robbed a bank?'

'I don't know another way. Charley gave me the chance so I took it.'

'Who's Charley?'

'Carl. His real name's Charley Smith but he thinks Carl sounds better.' Snowy took the plates away and brought mugs of tea. 'Anything else you want?'

Eddie spoke casually. 'That's a nice camera over there. Could I have a look at it?'

Snowy went to the mantelpiece and picked up the camera.

'What are you doing with that?' asked Spike.

'The kid wants to play with it.'

'So he can take snapshots of us?'

Snowy turned the camera over and pressed the catch on the back. Eddie held his breath, but the camera opened just like a real one.

'No film in it!' said Snowy.

'Put it back!' It was Carl who spoke.

'Why?' asked Snowy.

'I told you the boy must be tied up at all times, except when absolutely necessary. Tie him up now.'

After a moment's silence Snowy put the camera back on the mantelpiece. 'If you say so, bossman.'

Eddie lay back wearily on the smelly mattress. As his teacher often said, 'Not good enough. Try harder.'

He continued to lie there, tied up, for hour after hour, day after day, listening to Spike reminiscing about friends who had pulled off spectacular and profitable 'jobs' of one kind or another. From what Eddie could make out most of Spike's friends, for all their cleverness, were either going to the stir, already in it, or just coming out of it.

Carl sat on his bed most of the time reading crime novels while Snowy lay staring at the ceiling. Les was allowed to leave the building from time to time to fetch food. He was the only one without 'form', which meant he was in less danger of being picked up for questioning.

Eddie wondered if Slade was in prison by now, or back on Alphadelt.

Every lunchtime and evening Janet went to the coffee bar in Hammond Street and carried on with her work because if she had stayed at home anxiety would have driven her mad. As it was, she thought of Eddie about once every minute of the day and often during the sleepless nights.

At ten o'clock one evening she saw Slade come in from the street. Their eyes met but neither showed any sign of recognition. He took a seat at a table shielded by a partition. She went over to him, raising her pad.

'What can I get for you, sir?' she enquired in a loud voice. Then, in an undertone, 'I thought you'd gone for good, back to your home.'

'I've been looking for Eddie.' Seeing her hopeful glance Slade shook his head. 'No luck.'

'The fish is off,' said Janet loudly. 'The coppers are still after you. And the reporters. One of them came in here today. A woman. From her accent I guess she works for a foreign paper. She said she'd pay me whatever I wanted if I'd put her in touch with you. I told her to get lost.' Janet raised her voice again. 'Hamburger and chips, or mixed grill?'

'Mixed grill, please.'

Janet swept off to the kitchen to fetch his mixed grill.

Slade was sipping coffee when a woman came in from the street, tall, slim, and elegantly dressed. She wore a small fur hat with a brooch on the front and a leather bag hung over her shoulder.

Janet was beside him in a moment. 'That's the reporter I was telling you about!' she whispered.

The woman went to the counter.

Slade stared at her, puzzled. 'I've seen her somewhere before,' he whispered. 'How can I get out of here without her seeing me?'

'This way,' said Janet.

Slade followed her into the kitchen. They passed through a haze of hamburgers and chips to a back door.

'Good luck,' she said as he hurried off down the street.

Eddie had counted to a thousand to keep himself

awake. He raised his head to look around the dark room. The men were all asleep. Carl's bed was pulled across the doorway so that no one could get out without waking him.

'Sid!' called Eddie softly.

The whites of Snowy's eyes glinted at him in the darkness.

'I've got cramp,' Eddie complained. 'In my legs. And my arms. It hurts. I can't go to sleep.'

Snowy hesitated.

'I can't scarper, can I?' said Eddie reasonably. 'Not with Carl lying there.'

Snowy untied the cords and Eddie sank back with relief. 'Thanks!'

He started counting again until Snowy's breathing was deep and even. Then he swung his legs over the side of the mattress and stood up. He was unsteady on his feet for lack of exercise. He took a careful step forward and a floorboard creaked. He froze for several seconds but no one woke.

He moved forward again, testing each board as he went, until he reached the mantelpiece. As Eddie picked up the camera Spike stirred on his bed. Eddie froze again, but Spike only turned over and lay still.

Eddie clutched his prize tightly. He wanted to use it right away but he didn't know if the time adjustment was set at fast or slow.

He returned to the mattress as softly as he had come, stepping over the creaky board. Then he drew a tattered blanket over his head to form a tent, pointed the camera at the wall and pressed the button. A purple light flashed briefly on the wall.

Satisfied, Eddie was about to throw off the blanket when the siren of a police car wailed in the distance.

Instinctively, every man in the room stirred at once.

'Get up, all of you!' shouted Carl.

Eddie stuffed the camera under a corner of the mattress as they threw themselves off their beds. The siren was coming closer.

Carl grabbed his gun and went to the nearest window, peering between the planks.

'Bring the boy!' he ordered.

Eddie put out a hand for the camera, ready to risk everything, but before he could reach it Snowy hauled him off the mattress.

They all listened, pale with tension, as the police car turned into the street.

'Give him to me!' said Carl. He took Eddie by the scruff of the neck, thrust the gun into his side and spoke to Snowy. 'Moment they stop outside, bash those planks out of the window and let 'em see him.'

Eddie felt his stomach turn somersaults. Did the cops know the risk they were taking with his health?

The noise of the siren reached its highest pitch immediately below the windows . . . and then carried on, growing fainter.

Eddie felt the pressure of the gun disappear as Carl relaxed. 'A false alarm, gentlemen!' he said.

Spike swore and Les slumped on to his bed.

Then Carl's smile faded. 'Why is this boy untied?'

'Because he got cramp in the night,' said Snowy.

The two men eyed one another. 'Tie him up again,' said Carl. 'And see that he stays tied. That's an order!'

EIGHT

Slade slipped on his sports jacket in the hotel bedroom ready to start another day's search for Eddie. According to the newspapers, the police had found the second getaway car abandoned and it was thought that the gang was hiding somewhere in Stanwyck. But where? Perhaps some empty building? Slade had examined many already with no success.

He realised, guiltily, that in order to avoid further arguments with CC he had not reported to Alphadelt since he left Janet's house. It was high time he let them know where he was. He took the audio-unit out of its bottle.

'Slade calling Control.'

A male voice answered immediately. 'Come in, Slade. We have been waiting for you to report. This is Control Assistant speaking.'

'Hello, CA,' said Slade. 'Can I speak to CC?'

'Control Commander is not available. She has been transferred to other duties.'

Slade felt even more guilty. Had CC been dismissed because of his refusal to obey orders?

'Please inform us at once of your location,' said CA.

'I'm in the Hamilton Hotel, Wexford Street, Stanwyck.'

'Hold on.' After a pause CA spoke again. 'Your time-scanner was taken from you at the bank. Have you recovered it yet?'

'No,' said Slade ruefully. 'The gang have still got it.'

'According to our records, the time-adjustment function has been used recently.'

Slade took a quick breath. 'Used? How? When?'

There was another pause while CA consulted his computer.

'A brief T.R.E. was registered on our equipment, about five hours ago, Earth time.'

A time-retarding exposure! Eddie (or someone) must have triggered a purple flash from the camera in the middle of the night. An idea occurred to him. 'CA, can you check the record and get a fix on it for me? Find out where it was five hours ago.'

'I can try, but a fix from this distance will not be very accurate.'

'As near as you can make it, please. It's very important.'

Slade waited as patiently as he could till CA spoke again. 'The computer has placed it on our satellite map of your area.'

Slade spread his own map of Stanwyck on the bed. 'Go ahead, please.'

'The scanner is somewhere ... south of a row of bridges with metal bars on top ... west of a narrow waterway.'

Slade stabbed his finger on the map where the railway viaduct crossed the canal. 'Got it!' he said triumphantly.

'Do not attempt to recover the scanner now,' said CA. 'You must remain where you are until further orders. Acknowledge, please ... Slade? I said acknowledge please...'

But Slade did not hear him. The audio unit was in his pocket and he was on his way down the stairs. He stepped out of the hotel foyer ... and caught sight of the woman reporter coming down the street towards the hotel, fur hat perched on her head, leather handbag swinging from her shoulder.

Slade stepped back again hastily. He dived down a passage and left the hotel by a rear exit. Then he headed fast towards the canal.

Les drained a mug of coffee and picked up his shopping bag. 'See you later,' he said, going out with the bag under his arm.

It was eleven o'clock. Snowy was lying on his bed. Carl was reading another crime story and Spike was muttering to himself because no one else wanted to listen to him.

Eddie's hands were untied so that he could sip his mug of coffee, and he was making it last as long as possible. There was no way, he decided, that he could unfasten his ankles. If he asked to go to the loo, Snowy would tie him up again as soon as they got back. But did his legs have to be untied? As long as his hands were free why shouldn't he bend his knees and hop to freedom?

Carl put down his book and sighed. 'Another sad ending,' he declared. 'The villain got caught.'

'It's cold in here,' grumbled Spike. 'Couldn't we light a fire?' He stopped, staring at the mantelpiece. 'Where's the camera?'

Eddie's heart thumped. This was it! As calmly as he could he put his mug on the floor and reached under the corner of the mattress.

Spike pointed. 'Hey, look! The kid's got it!'

Snowy looked round, saw the camera in Eddie's hands, and began to swing his legs over the side of the bed.

'Sorry, Sid,' said Eddie under his breath as he pressed the button. A lengthy purple flash enveloped Snowy, and his legs hovered over the floor, scarcely moving.

Eddie hunched his body and thrust himself to his feet.

'What d'you think you're doing?' demanded Spike. He started forward briskly but a second flash slowed him down to a crawl.

Eddie took his first hops, heading for the doorway, and Carl moved into his path. 'Stay where you are, young man, or I'll – '

A third flash and Carl's threat, whatever it was,

came out as a slow, meaningless growl. Eddie hopped around him. There was a big key in the old-fashioned doorlock. Eddie dragged it out as he went through, pulled the door shut and put the key back in the lock. To his great joy it turned with a rusty squeak.

Hooking the camera strap over his shoulder, Eddie used both hands on the banister rail to help him along the landing and down the stairs. A dozen hops across the hallway took him to the big front door. He turned the handle but it wouldn't open. A modern mortice lock had been fitted and this time there was no key.

'Don't panic!' he warned himself. He flopped on to the floor and tugged at the cord round his ankles.

Slow creaking from upstairs warned him that the men were moving about. For how long, he wondered, would their retarded time-curves last and how long would the locked door hold them?

His ankles free, Eddie ran down a passage beside the stairs into a large storage area. Tall windows at the back of the old warehouse overlooked the canal but they were barred. He found another door leading to the towpath but that was locked too.

Then he remembered Les. Sooner or later Les would come back with the shopping. He must have a key to let himself in, but how soon would that be? There was a simple way to find out.

Eddie ran back to the hallway, pointed the camera at the front door and turned the focus control to see the future. Fifteen minutes ahead ... twenty minutes ... thirty minutes ... Still the door remained shut.

Would Les never come back?

At forty-five minutes the big door shuddered as if hit by violent blows from outside. The old timber post began to splinter around the lock. Another massive shove burst it open.

Eddie's eyes widened as he gazed through the viewfinder. It was not Les but Slade who came running in from the street wearing a sports jacket and a floppy cap.

Slade stopped at the foot of the staircase and looked up at the landing in alarm. Eddie raised the camera to see what Slade was looking at. Carl was leaning over the banister rail, the gun in his hand. No sound came from the future but flame spitting from the muzzle showed that the gun was fired.

Eddie swung the camera downward.

Slade slumped to the floor and lay still ...

Eddie lowered the camera, trembling. It doesn't *have* to happen, he reminded himself quickly. He could change the time-curves. With the camera he could keep the gang at bay till after Slade arrived.

He looked up to the landing. The movements above were getting faster as the trapped men recovered their normal timescale. There were shouts and loud thumping on the door ... so loud that Eddie did not hear the footseps in the passage behind him until it was too late.

An arm curled round his throat and yanked his head back. With a cry he dropped the camera. It crashed on to the stone floor and instantly shattered into a thousand tiny fragments.

'What are you doing down here?' demanded Les in his ear.

Choking for breath, Eddie realised his mistake. Les used the back, not the front door.

Eddie lay on his mattress once again, bound hand and foot, and Carl stood over him, his usual calm shaken by rage. 'How did you do it?' he demanded. 'How did you move so fast?'

Eddie shook his head helplessly.

'Let me get at him!' said Spike, advancing on Eddie with hands outstretched.

'Cool it, Spike,' said Snowy, grabbing the little man and hauling him back.

Spike struggled in fury. 'Let me go you black———'

'That's enough, both of you!' said Carl.

'I want my loot,' said Spike vehemently. 'I'm not staying here with that kid, or him –' he glowered at Snowy, '– or any of you any longer.'

'Maybe that's a good idea,' said Snowy, agreeing with Spike for once.

'If one goes, we all go,' said Les mournfully.

Carl nodded, accepting the inevitable. 'I'll get the money,' he said.

They waited in strained silence till he came back with the security box. 'Your job, Spike,' he said quietly.

Spike fetched tools from a suitcase by his bed. It took him only a few minutes to pick the lock on the case and remove a paint-spray device from inside. Then he opened the lid to reveal bundles of bank-notes.

Carl counted the money out in four piles. 'We leave here one at a time at ten-minute intervals,' he said.

'He's got to be snuffed,' said Spike, pointing at Eddie. 'Or he'll give 'em descriptions, the lot.'

Snowy was about to speak but Carl raised his hand. 'Not here, not now. I'll take him with me. I'll hold him for another three days to give the rest of you time to get clear. Then I'll dispose of him.'

Eddie shuddered.

'Since I have to deal with him I shall leave first,' added Carl. 'Untie him.'

While Snowy was releasing the cords Eddie saw the gun pointing at him and Carl spoke with icy coolness. 'I shall use this instantly if you try any more of your tricks.'

Eddie believed him.

Before anyone could speak again there was a loud crash from the hallway below.

For an instant the men froze and Eddie glanced at his watch. The forty-five minutes were up! Slade was battering on the front door.

'Wait there!' ordered Carl. He marched out of the room on to the landing, the gun in his hand. Snowy put a hand on Eddie's shoulder, more for protection than restraint.

With a final crash the front door burst open.

With a quick twist of his body Eddie ducked out of

Snowy's grip and ran. Before the others could move, he was out of the door on to the landing.

Carl was aiming the gun over the banister. Without slackening his pace Eddie hurled himself at the man's back, pitching him forward.

The gun fired but the bullet ploughed harmlessly into the staircase. Slade stepped swiftly backwards.

Moved by a blind desire to escape, Eddie plunged down the stairs three or four at a time. He was leaping down the last flight when Carl fired the gun a second time.

Eddie pitched forward as if hit by a hammer and sprawled on the floor at the foot of the stairs. Blood oozed from a wound in his back. Slade ran forward and dragged him out of the line of fire.

Carl started down the stairs with the other three men close behind him.

And then the strangest thing of all happened. The hallway was lit with a flash of white light, bright as a magnesium flare. When it was gone the men on the staircase were halted, frozen in their tracks, like four waxworks.

Slade looked round in astonishment.

The woman reporter was standing in the open doorway, pointing what seemed to be a scent spray at the staircase. Calmly she dropped it into her shoulder-bag and looked down at Slade.

'Found you at last!' she said. 'I see you are still making interference in Earth affairs.'

'CC!' gasped Slade. 'It's *you*!'

NINE

An ambulance arrived within minutes, pulling up at
the entrance of the warehouse. Slade came out of the
building with Eddie in his arms and got into it. CC
followed him.

As it drove away police cars appeared at speed and
screeched to a halt in front of the warehouse. Two
men crouched with guns pointing at the entrance
while the rest dived for cover.

Using a loud-hailer, Inspector Rowse invited the
gang to come out with their hands up but there was
no response. He approached the open door cautiously and peeped inside.

'I couldn't believe my own eyes,' he reported later
to the Chief Inspector. 'Charley Smith and his mates
were standing on the staircase like so many statues.
Didn't bat an eyelid between them. In some kind of
trance, I guess. Soon as I saw Charley, I knew we'd got
the gang. Then they started to come alive, one by one.
Gave 'em a real shock to find us there putting the
bracelets on. Seems all they could remember was a
flash of light, then nothing at all. Don't make sense to
me.'

It didn't make sense to the Chief Inspector either.

When Rowse arrived at Stanwyck General Hospital Eddie was being wheeled out of the operating theatre where a bullet had been removed from his spine.

'He won't be conscious for some time,' warned the surgeon.

'I want to talk to the couple who brought him here,' said Rowse.

'I'm told they disappeared as soon as we took him in,' said the surgeon. 'We didn't get their names.'

That evening Janet was allowed to see Eddie, who had been put in a private room.

'Hello, Mum,' he said.

'How are you, love?' she asked, trying to smile as she sank into a chair by the bed.

'Don't feel any pain,' he said. 'Don't feel anything at all in my legs. Can't even move them. I'll be all right soon, won't I?'

'We'll ... we'll have to wait and see,' said Janet. The surgeon had already told her, with deep regret, that Eddie would never walk again.

'Have you seen Alf?' asked Eddie.

Janet nodded. 'He's here, in the hospital. He has to watch out because the police are looking for him. He told me he'd like to see you.'

'I'd like to see him.'

'How much longer must we wait here?' asked CC impatiently. 'My orders are to return with you to

Alphadelt as soon as possible.'

They were sitting in the hospital canteen, shielded by the serving counter, sipping cups of coffee like anxious relatives waiting to visit a loved one. They spoke very softly in their own musical tongue.

'I can't go till I've seen Eddie,' said Slade firmly.

CC shook her head impatiently. 'In my opinion your attempts to right every wrong on Earth are hopelessly misguided.'

Slade smiled. 'Haven't changed, have you, CC? Except for that human shape. No wonder I didn't recognise you at first. Was it your own idea to come here to fetch me?'

'If you must know, there was a Higher Directive.'

Slade looked surprised. 'You mean –?'

CC nodded. 'He's taking a special interest in your mission and he's anxious that you come to no harm.'

'I'm glad that the Great Alph cares about me.'

'He also cares about Alphadelt. He does not want Earth people to find out who and what you are.'

'Would it matter so much? I thought the plan was to establish relations with Earth in due course?'

'That plan has been changed in view of what you have discovered. These people are selfish, aggressive, unpredictable –'

'Not all of them, not all the time!' protested Slade.

'They cannot manage their societies without injustice and upheaval. They even threaten one another with extinction. They might threaten us if they could! It's agreed that we shall make no further move till

94

they show signs of improvement, if they ever do. I wish to return to Alphadelt before there is more trouble.'

'You can go now if you like. I'll follow you soon, I promise.'

'That's not possible,' said CC. 'In order to get me here quickly I was dropped by an expendable craft. We must go back together in your ship.'

Slade saw Janet coming towards them and rose to his feet.

'This is Janet Salter,' he said to CC. 'Janet, this lady is not a newspaper reporter after all. She is a colleague of mine ... from where I come from.'

'How do you do?' said Janet.

'How are you? Pleased to meet,' said CC stiffly in English.

'Eddie wants to see you, Alf,' said Janet. 'I think I can take you to his room without anyone knowing.'

CC rose too. 'I shall make with you accompaniment,' she declared.

Eddie looked up hopefully as the door opened and Janet peeped into the room. Seeing he was alone she beckoned and Slade hurried in with CC.

'Hello, Alf,' said Eddie.

'Hello, how are you, nice to meet,' said Slade, smiling.

Eddie grinned. 'Learnt a lot since we first met, haven't you?'

Slade nodded. 'I've learnt a lot about you, Eddie.

You are very human, very selfish, right?'

'You could say that,' agreed Eddie.

'Yet you risked your own life to save mine! How do you explain that?'

Eddie avoided his eye, as if embarrassed. 'I couldn't let them shoot you, could I?' he muttered. 'I had to do something!'

Slade turned to CC. 'You see? Could the Great Alph ask for more?'

'Perhaps there *is* hope for Earth people,' admitted CC.

'Who's this lady?' asked Eddie.

'This is Control Commander from Alphadelt.'

Eddie's eyes widened. 'CC!'

'She's come to fetch me, but I shan't leave until you're better.'

Eddie shifted his shoulders uncomfortably. 'Nothing you can do, Alf. It's my legs. It's like they aren't there any more.' He looked up at Janet. 'What have they told you, Mum? What did they say?'

Janet opened her mouth but didn't speak.

'Did they say I'll get better?' he enquired relentlessly.

Tears sprang to Janet's eyes and Eddie let his head fall back on the pillow in despair.

Slade spoke to CC in their own language. 'Where is your medikit? You must have brought one, in case *I* was injured.'

CC glared at him. 'You wish to make more interference?'

'Yes!' said Slade. 'And you're going to help me! Never mind the regulations. This boy has been crippled on my account. What would the Great Alph do if he were here?'

'Oh, very well!' CC opened her bag and took out what might have been a powder compact.

Slade pulled back the bedclothes and turned Eddie over on his face.

'Just lie still,' Slade commanded. He ripped the sticky dressing from Eddie's back to reveal the wound sewn with stitches. Janet watched anxiously but, like Eddie, she trusted Slade.

From inside the 'compact' CC took a small metal dome on the end of a pair of hairline wires. 'Put the regenerator over the wound,' she ordered.

Slade placed the dome on Eddie's back and CC turned a tiny knob.

'We are using rays which activate the cells in your spine,' said Slade, 'so they restore themselves to their original pattern.'

For some time nothing seemed to happen. Then Eddie cried out in triumph, 'A-h-h! I can feel something, Alf. I can *feel* it!'

The surgeon and Inspector Rowse walked down the long corridor, pushing the swing doors aside in their path.

'He can talk to you now,' said the surgeon, 'but he's still very weak. I've done everything I can, but I'm afraid he'll be in a wheelchair for the rest of his life.'

'Poor kid,' muttered Rowse.

A couple passed them going the other way, a young man with a floppy cap pulled down over his face, and an elegant woman in a fur hat.

'He's in here,' said the surgeon. 'Please try not to tire him.'

They walked in.

The surgeon let out a cry of incredulity. Rowse looked very puzzled.

The patient was turning somersaults on his bed. His mother was watching him with cries of joy.

Eddie saw the surgeon and stood upright. 'Hi, Doc!' he called. 'How am I doing?'

Inspector Rowse ran into the corridor and hailed a nurse. 'Come quickly, please!'

'Is the patient in trouble?' asked the nurse.

'No, but the doctor is,' said Rowse.

X-rays proved that Eddie's spinal column was healed, as if it had never been fractured, and the stitches were removed. Janet insisted he be released from the hospital since not even a specialist, hastily summoned, could find anything wrong with him.

Eddie and Janet were taken to the police station where Eddie made a statement. Inspector Rowse was not at all satisfied when it was done.

'How did Slade know that a robbery was going to take place?' he enquired.

Eddie thought for a moment. 'You'll have to ask

him.'

'How come you were there at the same time?'

'Coincidence,' said Eddie firmly.

Reporters were waiting outside the police station but Eddie and Janet refused to talk to them.

When they reached home they found Slade and CC waiting behind drawn curtains in the front room.

'I was afraid you might have gone,' said Eddie, delighted to see them.

'Go we cannot,' said CC stiffly.

'Why not?'

Slade nodded to the empty space in the corner of the room. 'My bag is not here.'

'I meant to tell you, Alf,' said Janet. 'The police searched this room. They tried to open your bag but they couldn't, so they took it away with them.'

'Is that bad?' asked Eddie.

'Very bad,' said Slade. 'That bag is my compacted timeship.'

TEN

The police car sped out of town.

'Where are you taking me?' asked Slade.

'I can't tell you that,' said Inspector Rowse.

'Don't you know where we're going?'

'Of course I do! I'm not permitted to tell you.'

'But I'll know when we get there, won't I?'

'That's not my business,' said Rowse, clinging to the small print of the Official Secrets Act.

'I only came to your copperhouse this morning to get my bag.'

'I can't help that. You're under arrest as an illegal immigrant, and there may be other charges.'

'What other?'

'Espionage!' said Rowse darkly.

Slade was wearing his yachting gear once more. The audio-unit was inside his cap and CA spoke in his ear. 'You're travelling due south. Your telecom is giving us a constant fix on your location. Control Commander is following you.'

The car turned into a lane that wound among fields and woods. At last they reached a gateway set in a long wall.

'MINISTRY OF DEFENCE
OFFICER TRAINING ESTABLISHMENT'

said a notice. Inside was a guard hut.

'This is where I leave you,' said Rowse thankfully. He signed some papers in the hut, got into his car and set off back to town.

Slade was escorted by two uniformed men up a long drive to a big Victorian mansion hidden from the road by trees. They waited in the entrance hall where several people in civilian clothes were passing to and fro.

A squat, burly man with greying hair, wearing a shapeless suit, came down the stairs.

'Good morning, Slade,' he said. 'My name is Arkwright. Come with me, please.'

With the guards at his back Slade had no choice. Arkwright took them to a lift, which Slade thought surprising since the house was only two storeys high. But the lift did not go up. It went down.

CA spoke fast. 'CC is close behind you. I'm losing contact because of ...' His voice faded away as the lift descended deep underground.

They emerged into a long passage. Efficient-looking men and women, some in uniforms, some in white coats, passed up and down. More home-like was the elderly lady pushing a tea trolley.

'What kind of training do they do here?' enquired Slade.

'Allow me to ask the questions,' said Arkwright.

He pressed some buttons beside a door and it slid open. 'Go in, please.' He nodded to the guards who remained in the passage.

Slade found himself in a large laboratory. A man and a woman, both in white coats, were waiting there. Various items of equipment were scattered about and the kit-bag lay on a table in the middle of the room.

'That is what I want!' he said. 'May I take it now?'

'No, you may not!' said Arkwright. 'You have a lot of explaining to do first. You'll oblige me by opening it, since we've been unable to do so.'

'It's not made to open,' said Slade, 'not the way you mean.'

Arkwright stared at him, frowning. 'What use is a bag that doesn't open?'

Slade did not reply.

'I warn you, you won't leave here until you answer my questions. What material is it made of and how is it manufactured?'

'Material?' repeated Slade vaguely.

'Material so dense it won't yield even to a laser cutter. Forgive our interest, but you must realise the importance of armour-plating as effective as this to any power waging war.'

'It is not intended for making war,' said Slade emphatically.

'You expect me to believe that?'

'It's true.'

Arkwright eyed him grimly. 'Who are you? Where

do you come from? Who are you working for?'

Slade looked thoughtfully at Arkwright, then at the two laboratory assistants.

'You can't fight your way out of here, Slade,' said Arkwright, guessing what was in his mind. 'That door can be opened only by someone who knows the code, and the guards are outside.'

Suddenly another voice spoke, in Slade's ear. 'Control Commander calling Slade. Can you hear me?'

'I can hear you,' said Slade, realising that CC must be very close, probably in the passage outside.

'I'm sure you can hear me,' said Arkwright.

'I am in front of the lift,' she said. 'Which room are you in?'

'On the right, half-way down the corridor,' said Slade.

'What are you talking about?' asked Arkwright suspiciously.

Slade saw some chairs in a corner near the door. 'If you wish me to talk, may we sit down?'

'Certainly,' said Arkwright, pleased.

Slade took a chair in the corner. 'A cup of coffee would be welcome too,' he suggested.

'Very welcome!' agreed Arkwright, sitting opposite Slade. 'I saw the trolley outside.' He nodded to the male assistant who went to the door and pressed buttons.

As soon as the door opened Slade shouted, 'CC!'

Arkwright stiffened and the assistant at the door

looked over his shoulder, bewildered.

Then a white light stabbed into the room. The two assistants, standing one behind the other, were both frozen at the first flash. A second pinned Arkwright in his chair.

CC stood in the doorway holding her scent spray. A smaller figure appeared behind her, muffled in a greatcoat with the collar turned up and a big hat pulled down over his eyes. He took off the hat and grinned at Slade.

'Eddie!' said Slade. 'What are you doing here?'

'I had to bring him,' explained CC. 'I don't understand about taxis and things.'

'Nobody's seen my face,' said Eddie cheerfully. 'They didn't get a chance.' He nodded at the scent spray. 'That white beam is a total time-stopper. Fantastic!'

'Do not make talk,' said CC impatiently. 'We must get out of here speedfully.'

Slade grabbed his kit-bag, slinging it over his shoulder, and they hurried out of the room.

In the corridor the two guards and several other people were standing like statues. There was a quaint tableau around the tea trolley where an unmoving queue faced an immobile tea-lady.

A man standing inside the lift gazed at them with unseeing eyes as they ascended to ground level. More statues decorated the entrance hall. A woman came down the stairs and stopped, about to cry out in alarm, but a flash from the scent spray froze the cry on her lips.

They walked briskly down the drive. Three uniformed men stood transfixed outside the guard hut, one of them holding a rifle.

'They didn't want to let us in,' Eddie explained.

Outside in the roadway was a minicab. The driver stood beside it with a hand held out.

'You've time-stopped him too!' said Slade.

'He kept on about money,' explained CC, 'and I don't have any.'

A wailing sound arose from the house behind the trees.

'That's an alarm,' said Eddie. 'There's people up at the house we didn't fix.'

'We must get away from here,' said Slade.

'Let us take this machine,' said CC. 'Slade, you will please take charge of it.'

Slade chucked his kit-bag into the back of the minicab and Eddie climbed in after it. Slade and CC got into the front seats.

'Now tell it to go,' said CC.

'Tell it? I think not.' Slade looked at Eddie for advice.

'Turn that!' said Eddie, pointing to the key in the ignition switch. Slade turned it and the engine started.

'Pull this back one space.' Eddie pointed to the control lever, thankful that the car was automatic. 'Now put your foot on the right-hand pedal.'

Eddie released the handbrake between the front seats and the car jerked forward.

'That's better,' said CC, 'but why is it heading for the wall?'

'Steer it!' yelled Eddie.

'How does one steer?' enquired Slade.

Eddie leaned forward, grabbed the steering wheel and turned it. The car slewed round, inches from the wall.

'Now we're heading for the trees,' observed CC.

'Doesn't it know where it's going?' asked Slade.

'Of course not,' cried Eddie, giving the wheel another tug. 'Put your hands on there!'

Slade moved the steering wheel experimentally and the cab swung from one side of the road to the other.

'Now I cotton!' said Slade.

A car appeared round a bend ahead of him.

'Keep to the left!' advised Eddie hastily.

There was a screech of tyres and Eddie opened his eyes. Somehow the other car had passed them.

'You're going too fast,' he warned, staring at the bend ahead.

'How do I stop?' asked Slade.

'Put your foot on the other pedal, the big one!'

Slade looked down at his feet.

'I think you are too late,' said CC thoughtfully.

Slade jammed his left foot down and all three were flung forward. The cab skidded round the corner on two wheels.

'You ought to fasten your seat belts,' said Eddie.

'Will that make it work better?' asked CC.

'No, but you might survive.'

As they rounded another bend, a tractor turned out of a farm gateway hauling a cart which blocked the lane. Slade braked.

'How can we go past that?' asked CC.

Eddie looked out of the rear window and caught a glimpse of a large white car speeding down the lane from the direction of the house.

'I think they're coming after us!' he warned.

'We'll take the other road,' decided Slade.

He swung the wheel with a flourish and the cab lurched through the gateway into the field, bouncing over deep ruts.

'This isn't a road,' sighed Eddie.

They were climbing a gentle slope towards a line of trees behind a deep ditch.

'Look out for the ditch!' Eddie closed his eyes again.

There was a loud rattle as the car crossed a row of planks.

'We're over,' said Slade.

They passed through the trees which screened them from the lane. Slade drove confidently over the brow of the hill. On the other side a steep hollow yawned in front of them.

Slade braked but it was too late. The cab slid into the hollow and buried its bonnet in loose earth.

'Is this the end of the road?' asked CC.

'It certainly is,' said Eddie.

Slade planted his kit-bag on a patch of level ground. 'How will you get home, Eddie?' he asked.

Eddie looked down the hill towards a main road in the distance. 'I'll go that way,' he said. 'I can thumb a lift or get a bus.'

'Control Commander calling Alphadelt,' said CC. 'We are ready for take-off. Please activate all systems.'

As they watched, the kit-bag began to bloom like a demented mushroom, throwing up a gleaming dome, which spread sideways and downwards till it reached the ground. A lip appeared around the lower edge.

'A flying cup and saucer,' murmured Eddie.

CC turned to him and for the first time her stern features softened into a smile. 'We make departure now. I am glad you are not harmed in spite of all things.'

He shook her hand gravely. She went to the time-craft and pressed a faint mark on the metal. A hatch cover slid back and she stepped inside.

Slade took the wad of banknotes from his jacket and handed it to Eddie. 'Can you find the cab driver when you get back to town?' he asked.

'Sure,' said Eddie.

'Please give him pay for all the damages, and keep what is left for yourself.'

'I don't want your money, Alf,' said Eddie softly

'If you refuse money you will upset all m

108

researches,' said Slade gravely.

Eddie grinned. 'Okay, I'll take it if it saves you aggro.'

He put the notes in his pocket. Slade put out his hand and Eddie shook it.

'Will you ever come back, Alf?'

'Who knows? It's not for me to say.'

Slade climbed into the ship and the hatch closed behind him. A moment later the saucer-like rim began to whirl. There was a hissing sound and a sharp breeze tugged at Eddie's legs.

The dome lifted slowly, turning lazily on its axis. For a moment it hung a few metres above Eddie's head. Then it slid sideways and vanished from his sight into another time.

Eddie waved good-bye to the empty air.

FOR THE BEST IN PAPERBACKS, LOOK FOR THE

In every corner of the world, on every subject under the sun, Penguin represents quality and variety – the very best in publishing today.

For complete information about books available from Penguin – including Pelicans, Puffins, Peregrines and Penguin Classics – and how to order them, write to us at the appropriate address below. Please note that for copyright reasons the selection of books varies from country to country.

In the United Kingdom: For a complete list of books available from Penguin in the U.K., please write to *Dept E.P., Penguin Books Ltd, Harmondsworth, Middlesex, UB7 0DA*

In the United States: For a complete list of books available from Penguin in the U.S., please write to *Dept BA, Penguin, 299 Murray Hill Parkway, East Rutherford, New Jersey 07073*

In Canada: For a complete list of books available from Penguin in Canada, please write to *Penguin Books Canada Ltd, 2801 John Street, Markham, Ontario L3R 1B4*

In Australia: For a complete list of books available from Penguin in Australia, please write to the *Marketing Department, Penguin Books Australia Ltd, P.O. Box 257, Ringwood, Victoria 3134*

In New Zealand: For a complete list of books available from Penguin in New Zealand, please write to the *Marketing Department, Penguin Books (NZ) Ltd, Private Bag, Takapuna, Auckland 9*

In India: For a complete list of books available from Penguin, please write to *Penguin Overseas Ltd, 706 Eros Apartments, 56 Nehru Place, New Delhi, 110019*

In Holland: For a complete list of books available from Penguin in Holland, please write to *Penguin Books Nederland B.V., Postbus 195, NL–1380AD Weesp, Netherlands*

In Germany: For a complete list of books available from Penguin, please write to *Penguin Books Ltd, Friedrichstrasse 10 – 12, D–6000 Frankfurt Main 1, Federal Republic of Germany*

In Spain: For a complete list of books available from Penguin in Spain, please write to *Longman Penguin España, Calle San Nicolas 15, E–28013 Madrid, Spain*